BEST

Sir Michael Bichard
Sir John Tusa
Lord Karan Bilimoria
Sir Digby Jones
Dianne Thompson
Andy Green

As told to
Ed Peppitt

Hodder Arnold

A MEMBER OF THE HODDER HEADLINE GROUP

3849 ✓

The publisher has used its best endeavours to ensure that the URLs for external websites referred to in this book are correct and active at the time of going to press. However, the publisher and the author have no responsibility for the websites and can make no guarantee that a site will remain live or that the content will remain relevant, decent or appropriate.

For UK order enquiries: please contact Bookpoint Ltd, 130 Milton Park, Abingdon, Oxon, OX14 4SB. Telephone: +44 (0) 1235 827720. Fax: +44 (0) 1235 400454. Lines are open 09.00–17.00, Monday to Saturday, with a 24-hour message answering service. Details about our titles and how to order are available at www.teachyourself.co.uk

British Library Cataloguing in Publication Data: a catalogue record for this title is available from the British Library.

ISBN 978 0 340 942154

First published in UK 2007 by Hodder Education, 338 Euston Road, London, NW1 3BH in association with the Chartered Management Institute.

Typeset by Transet Limited, Coventry, England.
Printed in Great Britain for Hodder Education, a division of Hodder Headline, 338 Euston Road, London, NW1 3BH, by Cox & Wyman Ltd, Reading, Berkshire.

Hodder Headline's policy is to use papers that are natural, renewable and recyclable products and made from wood grown in sustainable forests. The logging and manufacturing processes are expected to conform to the environmental regulations of the country of origin.

Impression number   10 9 8 7 6 5 4 3 2 1
Year   2011 2010 2009 2008 2007

The Chartered Management Institute

chartered
management
institute

inspiring leaders

The Chartered Management Institute is the only chartered professional body that is dedicated to management and leadership. We are committed to raising the performance of business by championing management.

We represent 71,000 individual managers and have 450 corporate members. Within the Institute there are also a number of distinct specialisms, including the Institute of Management Consultancy and Women in Management Network.

We exist to help managers tackle the management challenges they face on a daily basis by raising the standard of management in the UK. We are here to help individuals become better managers and companies develop better managers.

We do this through a wide range of products and services, from practical management checklists to tailored training and qualifications. We produce research on the latest 'hot' management issues, provide a vast array of useful information through our online management information centre, as well as offering consultancy services and career information.

You can access these resources 'off the shelf' or we can provide solutions just for you. Our range of products and services are designed to ensure companies and managers develop their potential and excel. Whether you are at the start of your career or a proven performer in the boardroom, we have something for you.

We engage policy makers and opinion formers and, as the leading authority on management, we're regularly consulted on a range of management issues. Through our in-depth research and regular policy surveys of members, we have a deep understanding of the latest management trends

For more information visit our website **www.managers.org.uk** or call us on **01536 207307**.

chartered
management
institute

inspiring leaders

Chartered Manager

Transform the way you work

The Chartered Management Institute's Chartered Manager award is the ultimate accolade for practising professional managers. Designed to transform the way you think about your work and how you add value to your organisation, as it is based on demonstrating measurable impact.

This unique award proves your ability to make a real difference in the workplace.

Chartered Manager focuses on the six vital business skills of:

- Leading people
- Managing change
- Meeting customer needs
- Managing information and knowledge
- Managing activities and resources
- Managing yourself

Transform your organisation

There is a clear and well established link between good management and improved organisational performance. Recognising this, the Chartered Manager scheme requires individuals to demonstrate how they are applying their leadership and change management skills to make significant impact within their organisation.

Transform your career

Whatever career stage a manager is at Chartered Manager will set them apart. Chartered Manager has proven to be a stimulus to career progression, either via recognition by their current employer or through the motivation to move on to more challenging roles with new employers.

But don't take just our word for it…

Chartered Manager has transformed the careers and organisations of managers in all sectors.

- *"Being a Chartered Manager was one of the main contributing factors which led to my recent promotion."*
  Lloyd Ross, Programme Delivery Manager, British Nuclear Fuels

- *"I am quite sure that a part of the reason for my success in achieving my appointment was due to my Chartered Manager award which provided excellent, independent, evidence that I was a high quality manager."*
  Donaree Marshall, Head of Programme Management Office,
  Water Service, Belfast

- *"The whole process has been very positive, giving me confidence in my strengths as a manager but also helping me to identify the areas of my skills that I want to develop. I am delighted and proud to have the accolade of Chartered Manager."*
  Allen Hudson, School Support Services Manager,
  Dudley Metropolitan County Council

- *"As we are in a time of profound change, I believe that I have, as a result of my change management skills been able to provide leadership to my staff. Indeed, I took over three teams and carefully built an integrated team, which is beginning to perform really well. I believe that the process I went through to gain Chartered Manager Status assisted me in achieving this and consequently was of considerable benefit to my organisation."*
  George Smart, SPO and D/Head of Resettlement,
  HM Prison Swaleside

To find out more or to request further information please visit our website **www.managers.org.uk/cmgr** or call us on **01536 207429**.

Contents

Introduction by Ed Peppitt

Another book about management?

Yet another book about management? I knew, before I agreed to write this book, that the shelves were groaning with books about management. So why did I so readily take up the challenge to write this book, and what makes it so different?

Fundamentally, this book is the result of face-to-face interviews that I recorded with six of the UK's most effective and successful business leaders. It has given me a unique opportunity to meet and learn from some of the most influential people behind British business today and to capture their words on the printed page. So you are reading first-hand advice, tips and suggestions straight from the people most qualified to provide them.

But it's about more than a few suggestions about how to be a good manager. This book gets to the heart of British management and leadership, and the interviews reveal something of the personality and character of the people behind them. We wanted to write a book that was helpful, practical but also interesting to read. Advice is all very well, but it comes alive when supported by anecdotes and stories that place the advice in context. This book goes to the heart of the central aspects of modern management:

- Learn about meeting your customers' needs on a budget from someone who delivered cases of beer to restaurants in his battered 2CV.
- Hear about how to manage a crisis from someone who had to fix the country's network of broken payphones in six weeks.
- Learn about the importance of cascading information through an organization from someone whose staff only found out what was happening by watching the news on television.
- Hear about managing stress from someone who has learned to take time out to relax, even if it means having to watch four episodes of Spooks back to back!
- Hear about someone who learned to deal with difficult situations by sitting at the front desk of the Harlesden Benefits Office in order to appreciate the nature of the problems that he and his staff faced.
- Learn about the importance of planning from someone whose grand, strategic plan would never have been approved by management consultants yet he still managed to deliver it!

The business leaders

All six of the business leaders interviewed are Companions of the Chartered Management Institute. While writing this book, several colleagues and friends asked me what a 'Companion of the Chartered Management Institute' actually was. It's a fair question, so I made sure that I researched and prepared my answer at an early stage. Companions are the highest and most exclusive members of the Chartered Management Institute. You have to be invited to become a Companion, and you are only invited once you have demonstrated outstanding management and leadership achievement, over a sustained period, in substantial organizations. So it's a pretty exclusive club, not least because once invited to become a Companion, you even have to pay for the privilege.

The membership criteria are significant because of who might be excluded, rather than included. Since Companions must have demonstrated management and leadership skills over an extended period, many of the high-profile, get-rich-quick business celebrities are not amongst their number. Such celebrities might have simply hit upon a successful formula, and may not have employed model management or leadership skills. Companions, says the Chartered Management Institute, should be role models of the very best management and leadership skills. They must have made an impact in their chosen field, but that doesn't mean that everyone will recognize them from their television performances.

There are currently around one thousand Companions, and their accumulated experience represents a valuable resource of ideas and techniques that have proved their worth in driving organizations to success. They are role models for the next generation of managers, helping to encourage learning, development and good practice throughout the profession. They work with the Chartered Management Institute to help to raise the standard and status of professional management.

From the list of a thousand Companions, we chose six of the best. We wanted contributors from a range of sectors, with specific experience of the topics that we planned to discuss. So within these pages, you will hear from leaders in fields including business, industry, education and the arts:

Leading people: Sir Michael Bichard
Rector of the University of the Arts, London; Chairman of the Soham Murder Inquiry (2004); Permanent Secretary of the Department for Education and Employment (1995–2001); Chief Executive of the Benefits Agency (1990–5).

Managing change: Sir John Tusa
Managing Director of the Barbican Arts Centre, London (1995–current); Managing Director of the BBC World Service (1986–93).

Meeting customer needs: Lord Karan Bilimoria
Founder and Chief Executive of Cobra Beer Ltd; Chairman of the National Employment Panel's Small and Medium Sized Enterprise (SME) Board.

Managing information and knowledge: Sir Digby Jones
UK Skills Envoy; Former Director-General of the CBI; Chairman of the Industries Strategy Group of Deloittes; Senior Advisor to Barclays Capital; Special Advisor to Ford of Europe.

Managing activities and resources: Dianne Thompson

Chief Executive of Camelot Group Plc, operator of the UK National Lottery.

Managing yourself: Andy Green

Chief Executive, BT Global; Chief Executive of BT Openworld (1996–2001).

All six of our Companions have demonstrated outstanding leadership skills in their chosen field, and were matched, as closely as possible, with the subject on which they agreed to talk. **Sir Michael Bichard** led a team of 30,000 at the Benefits Agency, as well as a much smaller team during the harrowing Soham Murder Inquiry – there can be few people more qualified to talk about leading people than him. **Sir John Tusa** is certainly qualified to talk about managing change, having spent ten years transforming the Barbican Arts Centre from a dysfunctional, crisis-ridden and unloved venue into the unified, profitable and spectacular arts complex that it is today. Who better to talk about meeting customer needs than **Lord Karan Bilimoria**? In little more than ten years, he has built Cobra Beer from scratch, a global beer brand with a £10 billion turnover. **Sir Digby Jones** may not be the world's most prolific user of IT, but as Director-General of the CBI for the last seven years he has witnessed the UK's transformation into a knowledge economy, so he is the ideal spokesperson for a discussion about managing information and knowledge. As Chief Executive of Camelot, **Dianne Thompson** manages the UK's National Lottery. With Camelot receiving less than half a pence profit from every pound spent on the lottery, Dianne certainly has plenty to say about how to monitor and manage every single resource at her disposal. And, finally, there is BT Global's Chief Executive, **Andy Green** – quite simply, Andy has demonstrated a calmness and professional approach to his leadership that he has developed by taking control of his time, as well as his physical and mental wellbeing. Whole books have been written about how to manage yourself, and their authors probably had someone like Andy Green in mind when they wrote them.

So what makes this book different?

Above all, this book is different because it looks at management and leadership as a whole. It's noteworthy, I think, that most management books tend to fall into one of three categories:

1. **Books about a single management discipline.** I am not disputing that a book about managing time effectively can be useful. So can a book about managing a budget, people or projects. However, such books are often too simplistic. If, as a manager, you fail to manage your time effectively, there may be all sorts of reasons for this. It may have very little to do with how well you plan your day, set your agenda, list your tasks and goals, and all the other routines that books on time management tend to recommend. It is just as likely to do with how effective you are as a manager, per se.

   When I was a newly appointed sales and marketing manager for a publishing company in London, I was sure that I needed help with prioritizing my workload and managing my time. I attended a number of time management courses, applied their techniques, and saw little improvement in my performance. It was some time later that I began to appreciate that my time management skills were not at fault, and that my issues could be attributed to the fact that I had failed to change my attitude or approach as I had risen through the ranks of the company. Andy Green has a lot to say about this issue in chapter 6.

2. **Academic management books.** Management theory is valuable, though it doesn't always make for great reading. We wanted to publish a book that provides valuable and interesting insights into how effective managers operate. There's no management theory in this book at all – but there are loads of examples, anecdotes and stories that illustrate many management principles, straight from the mouths of the leaders of some of our best known organizations.

3. **Business biographies.** Biographies of well known businesspeople make fantastic, entertaining reading. It's fascinating to learn how a well known person in business made it to the top. Having said that, such books are rarely full of lessons that the average person in business can apply to their own situation – they are usually the stuff of dreams, albeit entertaining ones. My hope for this book is that it provides much of the interest of a business biography, coupled with genuine and practical advice and help that you can take away and apply in your organization and in your life. I have learned a great deal myself, and I hope that you will too.

So, this book is set apart from other management books because it looks at management and leadership as a whole, based on the actual experiences of some the UK's top business managers and leaders. And while we are about it, let's dispel one myth forever. There is a tendency to consider *management* and *leadership* as two distant family members, with management the poor relation. It's as if management is the boring stuff that you have to get under your belt before you can get on and learn how to be a leader.

If this book delivers nothing else, I hope that what comes across is that management and leadership go hand in hand. Each one of the six leaders I met are, first and foremost, exceedingly accomplished managers. True, not everyone who can manage a budget can manage a team – but anyone who has studied and gained experience of the six management principles in this book is ready to lead.

Who is this book for?

That's a great question! The book was inspired by the Chartered Management Institute's own Chartered Management Programme, which is a learning programme designed for middle and senior managers. So at one level, this book is written specifically for them. It might encourage them to think about studying for the programme themselves, or at the very least to offer them first-hand and practical lessons that they can apply in their own management and leadership careers.

Having mentioned the Chartered Management Programme, this book has a far wider audience. Business television programmes like 'The Apprentice' and 'Dragons' Den' may attract substantial audiences, but they hardly represent an accurate picture of what businesses, and the people who run them, are all about. As one of my interviewees has said about 'The Apprentice', 'It puts business in a very bad light. Young people will be turned off because they think they will be shouted at by a horrible, fat, old, rich bloke'. If you are keen to find out which of the six Companions said that, then this book is for you.

This is a bedside book for anyone interested in business, and the people behind it. If you want to know what the UK's most effective leaders are like as people, rather than as decision makers, then read on. Naturally, these interviews touch on how each leader has reached their current position, but they spend much more time on their values, their hopes and their expectations. If you've ever thought that the television portrayal of a brash, authoritative, aggressive business leader is an accurate one, then prepare to be surprised.

This is a book for all of us. It's not a blueprint for how to succeed in business or, indeed, in life. Rather it provides an insight into the working lives of a handful of our most successful leaders. Above all, it teaches us that management is not a dull term, usually prefixed with words such as 'financial' or 'human resources'. Management, together with leadership, are challenging, engaging and rewarding careers in themselves. These six personalities are absolutely passionate about what they do, and that passion rubs off on those around them. I hate to break this to you, but here are six people whose message is that management is fun!

01

Sir Michael Bichard on leading people

Sir Michael Bichard, Rector of the University of the Arts in London

'The most exciting thing of all in leadership, I think, is to get to the point where people are using their own initiative to deliver.'

Sir Michael Bichard has worked in the public sector throughout his career, with 20 years in local government and nearly ten in central government. He was Chief Executive of two local authorities, Brent and Gloucestershire, and in 1990 became Chief Executive of the Benefits Agency, with 65,000 staff and an administrative budget of £2.5 million.

He was recruited as Permanent Secretary of the Employment Department in 1995 and became Permanent Secretary of the merged Department for Education and Employment later that year. In May 2001 Sir Michael left the civil service, and in September 2001, was appointed Rector of the London Institute, which in May 2004 became University of the Arts London. As Rector, he is responsible for the largest art and design institute in Europe and for its six constituent colleges – Chelsea College of Art and Design, London College of Fashion, London College of Communication, Central Saint Martins College of Art and Design and Camberwell College of Arts.

Throughout his career, he has been interested in the management of people and performance, leadership, equality, customer service and quality. Whilst Permanent Secretary, he had responsibility for three of the government's main objectives: raising standards in schools, creating a learning society and moving people from welfare to work via the New Deal.

Sir Michael is a Governor of Henley Management College, a Member of the Board of Companions of the Chartered Management Institute and a Member of the Guild of Educators. In January 2004 he was appointed by the Home Office to chair the inquiry into the Soham murders. He received a knighthood in the Queen's Birthday Honours 1999.

There is an awful lot written about how to lead people. Entire sections in the bookshop are dedicated to leadership, motivation and the distinction between managing and leading a team of people.

My brief was to meet and talk to someone who had led teams of people effectively throughout their career. Who better qualified than Sir Michael Bichard, who as Chief Executive of the Benefits Agency had led a team of 65,000 staff? If anyone could explain what leading people was about, it would be him.

As I arrived at the University of the Arts London, where Sir Michael is Rector, I read the Chartered Management Institute's own summary of what leading people means:

> 'The increasing role of values, communication and interpersonal relationships have emphasised the growing complexity of leadership in today's dynamic workplaces. But leadership is not just expected from those at the top of an organisation. Increasingly, it is a challenge for all, especially as many organisations have become flatter and less hierarchical.'

Would Sir Michael agree with this statement? Just what are the skills that make up a good leader? How should successful leadership be defined – simply by the goals achieved by an organization, or is there more to it than that? Does good leadership depend on the decisions and judgments made by an individual, or the circumstances they are made in? I jotted these questions down, along with many others, as I sat down in Sir Michael's office.

Vision, values and taking ownership

I began the interview by reading the quotation from the Chartered Management Institute. Did Sir Michael Bichard agree that leadership was all about values, communication and interpersonal relationships?

It is certainly one way of covering the issue. I think as a leader, particularly in large organizations, my aim has always been to try to create a sense of purpose and direction. I think there are two particular things that enable you to do that. One is to get some ownership for a clear business vision – you need to know where the business or organization is going. The other is to get a sense of ownership for a clear set of values. For me, values have always been as important as the business vision, because values are about behaviour. So what I am trying to do is not just get clarity about where the business is going, but also about how the people in the business are going to behave together.

So leadership is about vision and values?

Yes. And ownership, because lots of organizations say they've got a vision, and some say they've got values. But if people in the organization don't recognize that they have some ownership of the vision and values, then they don't have any effect on the way the organization works. However, if you get it right it can be a driving force. When I was in the Benefits Agency, we did a lot of work on the values there. We had just three or four values. You could go to any office in the country and they would tell you what the values were. Then gradually you could see people interpreting the values in their own way. For example, one of the values was customer service and quality. They began to develop their own take on that, using their own initiatives. But basically you have still got to have clarity and ownership of vision and values at the outset.

So it was a good thing that people were interpreting the values in their own way?

Oh yes, absolutely. The most exciting thing of all in leadership, I think, is to get to the point where people are using their own initiative to deliver. They won't always do it in exactly the way you would have done, but I think one of the tasks of leaders sometimes is just to step back and stop making people do things the way you would do them.

You mentioned the Benefits Agency earlier, and I read that you had overall control of 65,000 people. With an organization with such a massive head count, where did you begin, how did you start?

It was being set up as a new organization, so it was the biggest of the government's Next Step agencies. The staff came from the DSS, the Department of Social Security. They were being set up as a separate entity with its own kind of identity, its own pride. So I had an opportunity not to start completely afresh, but to think radically about what kind of organization it wanted to be.

At the time, the staff had been taught that customers weren't that important, and that quality wasn't that important. This was an opportunity to say that customer service and quality were both very important. A lot of people in the organization just wanted to be liberated, just wanted to be told by the leader that actually these things really did matter and they could then get on and use their initiative to improve the quality.

I can see how, as a new department, the vision was there from the outset. But what about the values? Where did they come from? Were they your values?

I think any leader has a set of values. I think what you need to do is to take your values to the organization and make them clear. At your initial job interview, if necessary. Because I think if you go to an organization where your values are not welcome, you may get through the interview, but actually what you will end up doing is having hell for four or five years because you will constantly be fighting a group of people in an organization that don't share your basic values.

I have basic values around the way I treat people and respect people. I have basic values around what I think of clients and customers, and how I expect people to be treated and the importance of service. I try to make those clear at the outset. I think when you then engage with the organization you probably adjust and adapt your values, so you may express them in slightly different ways. You may emphasize one of your values at a particular time and emphasize another at another time, but if you are a leader trying to lead an organization in a way which is not compatible with your basic values, then it is not going to work.

I think leaders have to be natural. They have to be themselves. I mean, there are different sorts of leaders, some of them are introverts, some of them are extroverts – but the leaders I have always respected are the people who are being themselves. You can't be yourself if you are trying to pretend that the values of the organization are your values, or vice versa.

So if you had been head-hunted, or you are applying for a job of some sort of leadership role in an organization, and you know perfectly well that their values aren't yours, what should you do?

You don't go there. I think one of the other things that all of the leaders I respect have had is a passion and a belief in what they are doing in the organization, in the product, in the service.

I always say to young people, on speech days and at degree ceremonies, for God's sake don't get yourself into a position where you don't feel passionate about what you are doing. Because again, it is not something you can pretend. People know whether you believe in what you are doing in the organization. If they don't believe that their leader is passionate and has belief, then what chance do you have that they will?

Is that part of the difference, do you think, between a manager and a leader?

Everyone always asks me, what is the difference is between management and leadership? I am not a great reader, but the best definition I know is by John Kotter, an American academic, who talks about *management* in terms of planning, budgeting, monitoring, identifying issues, resolving issues and evaluating. By contrast, *leadership* is about creating this sense of purpose and direction. It's about getting ownership, getting people aligned to it, and it is actually about getting people to believe they can achieve it. And that's very different. I think you can sustain an organization in reasonably stable times through good management. But transforming an organization takes real leadership, and not leadership just at the top of the organization: it is about getting leadership right the way through the organization. I talk to people who may only have four or five people working for them, but they are leading that team – and how effective that team is depends very much upon the quality of their leadership.

And what's the process for identifying potential leaders of smaller teams throughout an organization, and then getting them to take ownership of the values and the direction?

You have got to spend a lot of time getting people involved in the discussion about the vision and the values. In this university, about a year ago, we spent several months talking to as many staff as we could about what our strategy should be in the medium term, and what kind of place we wanted this university to be. A university is not the easiest place to do that because people are not used to that kind of debate. Many just want to teach and research, and leave the management issues to others. But it was a really positive exercise.

That's exactly what we did in the Benefits Agency as well. I spent the first six months in the Benefits Agency visiting and talking to people personally about the values we wanted, what we believed in, the things that would make us a successful organization. That's part of the process of getting ownership. I mean, if people across the organization don't own the vision, then it is not going to happen. They won't all take ownership, but you have to get a critical mass.

That is very interesting. And, from your experience, does that process tend to identify people who realize that their values don't match up to those of the organization that they work for?

Absolutely. I always take the view that if someone leaves the organization, particularly if they are in a senior position, then that's a failure, in that you want people to be part of the organization. But there are clearly times when there is a mismatch, and when you have to part company with someone. When you get to that point, I have never seen any reason to treat individuals with anything less than dignity. After all, some people have been brought up to work in a particular way for 25 years, because that's what's been wanted from them in the past. It would be very arrogant of someone to come in and say, 'Well actually I want to do something completely different and we don't need you any more'. You need to try to give people the opportunity to be a part of the change – but if they can't, then you need to help them to find something else.

Communication

I was starting to build a clear picture in my mind of Sir Michael Bichard's approach to leading teams. Sharing the organization's vision, and its values, forms the basis of this approach. But sharing the vision and the values only benefits an organization if its people are given genuine ownership of them. That means that an organization must involve its people from the outset, rather than simply hand them the latest strategic direction policy document.

I understood the theory, but how do you communicate or share a vision throughout an organization, particularly one the size of, for example, the Benefits Agency? I needed to probe deeper.

So, if we consider the vision for a moment, how is it communicated across this university? Or throughout the Benefits Agency? Is it simply a case of talking to people, as you mentioned, or are you publicizing it in any other way?

I think the way in which you communicate effectively depends upon the size of the organization. It is a bit like talking to an audience. If I am talking to an audience of ten people then I adopt a very different style than if I am talking to an audience of 500 people. If you are running the Benefits Agency with 500 offices and 65,000 staff, you know you are going to adopt a different strategy for communication than if you are running a much smaller organization. I don't think there's a science. I think you have got to keep changing the way in which you communicate, because communications can become very routine and then people don't listen.

So you have got to adopt a whole panoply of different strategies. They need to include some personal visibility, and that's not easy when you are dealing with 500 offices. I've seen people torture themselves running national organizations by trying always to be up front and spending their whole week on a train. You can't do that, but you have got to show some personal visibility. Fortunately, with technology now you can do it in all sorts of other ways, such as emails and websites. I used to put my diary on the web so that people could see what I was doing for the next couple of weeks and what I thought were important issues. For a smaller organization, I would adopt a rather more intimate style, such as coffee mornings, tea-breaks, lunches. I used to advertise that I would be in the building, and available, at ten o'clock on Wednesdays if people wanted to come and have a chat.

I think that there are two important things in communication. One is, it isn't just about telling, it really is about listening. The other thing is getting the balance right between being consistent without being rigid. People don't want the message to change fundamentally every week, particularly if you are trying to change an organization. So the fundamental message has got to be consistent. If you say that this organization stands for caring for its staff, the quality of its service, the way it treats its customers and the value for money it provides, then you do not change those fundamental messages. Otherwise people just get totally confused, or de-energized. That's a mistake that a lot of managers and leaders make – they are constantly giving out different messages. So it's important to be consistent.

But if you are listening, then you can't be rigid, partly because you are learning things all the time, and partly because there are things going on which you must adapt to. So you have got to be flexible whilst remaining consistent.

Yes, I can see the importance of communication, particularly in a vast organization such as the Benefits Agency. But how do you set in motion the structures and methodologies that enable you to listen to the issues and concerns of so many different people?

I think you can start with some of the mechanisms I have talked a bit about already. It is not rocket science, frankly. If you are genuine about wanting to do it, there are all sorts of ways in which you can communicate with people. I think the question is whether the individual, the leader, has actually got the ability to communicate, really communicate, including listening and talking, with different people in different parts of the organization – put them at their ease, convince them that you really are listening and that you want to hear what they say, understanding, trying to get into their shoes. For me, communication is about trying to get in the shoes of the people you are talking to on the front line in the Toxteth Benefit Office. What kind of pressures are they are facing?

That sounds like rapport-building?

Yes, I think the rapport is putting people at their ease. I used to watch some permanent secretaries doing visits, and they would make a great thing about how they were in touch with the staff. Yet they would actually take four or five people with them and descend on an office, and everyone there was on edge. It was a sort of inspection tour. And you come away from that, and you haven't learned anything. People don't tell you what really is bothering them because they don't think you want to hear it.

What people really want is to be reassured that everything is OK. But what you have to do sometimes, if you want to improve the quality of service and if you really care about that as a leader, is to find out what's not working very well. And sometimes you discover that something you have suggested is part of the reason why it isn't working very well. You have to put people sufficiently at their ease for them to be able to say, 'Look, what really is getting us down is this'. But too many leaders don't want to hear that.

The Benefits Agency was a good example. For the first two years in the Benefits Agency, there was so much anger in that organization that when you went to visit Grimsby on a Friday, they wanted to sit you down and just tell you how angry they were. And sometimes I came away feeling hugely depressed and the only way I could keep going was to recognize that they thought I might do something about it, otherwise they wouldn't waste their time telling me. With some leaders, the staff just didn't think they were going to do anything, so they didn't waste their breath.

That is a stark picture. In those circumstances, did you feel that it was your responsibility to take away their anger? Or accept it but try and do something about it?

Well two things really. One is, if people tell you things that can be fixed, you fix them. You make sure that someone goes back and tells them what you've done, otherwise you have even lower credibility with them. I used to do phone-ins, which is slightly old technology now, but I would set aside a day when everyone would know that they could ring me and complain, or make points, and we had an arrangement whereby they always got a reply within three weeks. You have got to make sure you go back and respond to their concerns.

The other thing is to realize is that sometimes people just want to get something off their chests. Most people don't expect miracles, but they do think that the leader ought to be interested enough to let them let off steam from time to time. You have got to be resilient. Sometimes you have got to take that on the chin.

I believe that leaders earn huge credibility if people believe that they are trying to get rid of some of the obstacles that are stopping them doing a good job. And partly this is about finding out just what *is* stopping people doing a good job, because most people want to do a good job. They don't want to come and be a pain in the neck and they don't want to work for an organization that is unsuccessful. So if you can get across to people that you are really trying to find out what the obstacles are and that you want to do something about them, then they'll listen to you.

Motivation and creating energy

I was intrigued by the idea that a leader earns huge credibility by trying to get rid of some of the obstacles that are stopping people doing a good job. The combination of listening to what your people have to say, and then doing something about the things that stand in their way, is clearly empowering. Communication at this level is persuasive, but what else must a leader do to motivate a team? Having read so much about motivation, I found Sir Michael's response both challenging and refreshing.

I was going to ask you about motivating a team and motivating employees, and it sounds as if the process you have just described is the key?

I find that 'motivating' is not a word I warm to, really. In a way I find it slightly condescending, as if you are manipulating people.

The thing I am quite interested in, and have been for a while now, is creating energy, which is a different way of putting it. I think that one of the things that leaders can do most of all is to create and enhance energy in organizations, and it is one of the big distinctions, I think, between successful and unsuccessful leaders. I have seen people in leadership positions who stifle creativity and energy. I have visited many schools and workplaces in my time, and you don't need to be there very long to work out whether or not it is a place that has got buzz, energy, creativity, passion, or whether or not it is a really great place to be. Usually the reason for that is the person who is leading the team, the place, the school. So I think leaders need to think a lot more than they do about how you create energy.

I think one of the ways you create energy is get rid of some of the obstacles. Every organization has obstacles. Sometimes there are an excessive number of meetings, or a paper culture. In the Benefits Agency, there were endless audit checks. Everything that was done in that organization was checked by someone else. Every single decision. And this meant that the people who took the decisions thought that they weren't being valued because they were always going to be checked. And I thought, why on earth are we doing this? So we introduced a random checking procedure which achieved what we wanted but didn't involve quite such a bureaucratic process. So you try to get rid of the things that are concealing the energy, you try to get rid of the dysfunction.

A lot of leaders, I think, try to turn their back on some of the disagreements that are going on within the organization, either with individuals or between workplaces. But doing that drags down the energy levels of the organization.

So get rid of the things that conceal the energy and then try to think about ways in which you can create energy. One example is the way in which you personally go about things. For instance, if someone comes in here with an idea, you can either send them out feeling full of energy and enthusiasm, or you can tell them all the reasons why it won't happen. Or you can tell them 'We tried that in 1986', or 'We haven't got enough money', or 'Sorry, I'm really busy today' or 'It's good in theory but it's not going to work in practice' – you get the idea. If they go out and feel de-motivated, they will tell everybody else. They won't come to you with new ideas. The organization has lost a pocket of energy and has replaced it with someone who is just going to serve their time. So I think the way in which the leader behaves has a huge impact on whether the organization is passionate and has got energy.

That sounds great in theory. But if someone walks through your door here with an absolutely ridiculous idea in your opinion, what do you do then?

Well it depends on how ridiculous it is. I mean if someone comes through the door and has an idea which I think is silly, I would never say, 'That's a stupid idea'. What I would say is, 'Let's talk about it a bit more. How's it actually going to work in practice? How much is it going to cost? How is it going to fit in with some of the other things we are doing at the moment?' And you may well come to the conclusion, hopefully with that person, that this particular idea isn't going to work terribly well, but you have still sent them away knowing that you listened to them. It may not be a long conversation, but you can send them away with a sense that you were interested enough to have the conversation, and that if they had another idea they would bring it to you, rather than having demeaned them to the point where they would never come to you again.

The importance of teams

So rather than talking about motivating an individual person or motivating an individual team, it sounds to me as if the passion and the energy become infectious.

I think they do, and that's a reason why the snowball effect is important, because you have got to have the passion, you have got to have the energy, and your team around you have got to have it too. We haven't talked about teams, and I think one of the great skills of the most effective leaders is to get really effective teams around them.

So it's the recruitment of teams that is important?

Yes, recruit where you can, and gradually, if you take on a team that's already established then there will be changes over time, inevitably, and you have got to try to get around you a team that shares the values and the vision and really lives them. It's a bit of a cliché, but what the organization is always doing is watching that team and seeing whether or not they are reflecting what you say the organization is about, and how passionate they are. If they see that there are disagreements on fundamental issues, or people are talking down what you are trying to do behind your back, and you are not doing anything about it, then they assume that you are not serious and that the organization is not serious.

So getting a really strong team around you is very important.

How does that process begin?

If you are going into a ready-made team, it begins with an assessment of the people that are there. You need to be clear about where you are going and what kind of organization you want to be, and you need to make it clear that you are going to do that together, and you are going to involve the organization in it. Naturally, it may be that during the course of this process, one or two people don't share that vision or want to move on. Inevitably some people retire. Some people move on because they want to get promotion. There will be recruiting opportunities, and you have got to be clear about how you want to use those opportunities.

A great example was when we merged the departments for Education and Employment. It was a one-off opportunity really, so we took the decision that everyone was going to apply for the jobs, because everyone had to be sure that this was an honest process, and that no one was going to get the job just because they happened to have been in Education rather than Employment, or Employment rather than Education. The civil service often misses that kind of opportunity, because it doesn't have regard to attitudes, achievements or values – it appoints people on the basis of the jobs they have had in the past. I don't think that's enough. So we were pretty careful about the kind of people we appointed to that new board. Then we got one or two non-executive board members in as well, with the right set of skills, and the result was a fantastic board. As the leader of that board, your effectiveness is multiplied a thousand-fold because you have got eight or nine people there sharing the values, taking them through the organization. It's a fantastic feeling.

So when you have a good leader of a team or a department, are you tempted to leave them alone?

I often say that there's always enough going wrong in any organization not to waste your time interfering with people who are getting it right. So I think you are right. If I look back at some of the best people I have worked with, why would I want to second-guess every decision they were making? But I can be pretty interventionist if someone isn't getting it right!

Let's talk about that for a minute. Things aren't going right. Do you replace the leader?

Well, first you have got to have certain things in place. We have talked about the importance of vision and values. I think there is a clear sense of priorities in an organization which you only get through a decent business plan. When I came to the university, there was no business plan process at all. There was a budget and target numbers for recruiting students, and that was about it. We have got six colleges here, and that was about the extent of business planning. Now we have a business plan process. It has credibility. I meet with the management teams of each of the colleges twice a year and I review how they are doing against their key priorities and against any other issues that have come up during the course of the year. We take those meetings very seriously. The meetings will be two or three hours long. I used to do it in the Department and at the Benefits Agency, and obviously I meet the senior managers pretty regularly apart from those meetings.

So to be clear about whether or not a college is performing well, or whether the leader of that college is performing well, I think my first task is to support the leader and look at ways in which we can help and identify if there are issues that can be resolved. But as we said, there are occasions when you get to the point where you think that the person just can't hack it, they are not going to be able to turn this round. If that's the case, your responsibility is to the college, to the organization, and to the rest of the staff. You can't ignore the fact that the individual is damaging all of that, and so then I think you do have to look for ways in which you can respectfully part company and move on to something else.

You mentioned the business planning process a few minutes ago. Is it the role or the responsibility of the leader to develop the business plan?

Well I did, because that was a particular need that I felt we had and there was no one else who was going to do it. I think leadership is sometimes about adapting to different situations. For example, I was here with one of my chief executives just before you came in, and we were having a discussion about the extent to which he was 'hands-on'. We agreed that he was probably more hands-on than he would like to be. I was saying that I think sometimes that's inevitable. In the same way, I think that the business planning element here was inevitable and I've had to spend quite a lot of time on what is not strategic management, but operational management, because the skills weren't here. It was an important part of getting the university heading in the right direction. So I think you have got to be a bit flexible.

I would like to spend a little less time on business planning now, and spend more time on external relations and fund-raising, because the future of the university depends upon us getting more money which isn't government-related. So that's a new leadership task, in a way. You have got to be flexible.

Leadership across different organizations

Are the principles of leadership the same, regardless of the organization?

Yes I think they are. I think the core of leadership is about people, but I think you have got to be sensitive to the history, the traditions, the customs and the practice of your organization. I don't believe you can just go in headlong and impose your particular style on an organization. One of the reasons I came here was that I wanted to try my leadership style in a different setting with different people – in this case, creatives, artists and designers.

Regardless of the organization, though, one of the most difficult times for a leader is the first six months in a new organization.

Why do you think that is?

Because on the one hand you have to go through that stage of listening and learning about the organization, and quickly understanding the things that aren't working, as well as the things that it really feels passionate about. You have to make sure you don't step on a landmine. And so, in that sense, it is a time when you should be stepping back and listening.

But it is also the most powerful time you will ever get in the organization, because people will listen to what you have to say. They will try to interpret you, and you can send out the most powerful signals and messages in that first six months. For example, I'm not hierarchical, I am not status-conscious, and I wanted to get that message across to people. This university, when I came here, was very status-conscious and hierarchical. If you want to break that quickly, then that's the time to do it.

So you have got to balance those two things, and I think often what I try and do is to do some of my listening and learning before I even join an organization. It's not just by talking to people in the organization, either. Some of the most insightful comments about an organization come from people who are outside it, and who deal with it.

So it's important to do a lot of that learning, so that when you are in the building you actually know what the messages are that you want to send to that organization. My messages here are around, 'We're here to deliver a top-class service to clients that we really care about – in this case students. I really care about results and outcomes. I am not someone who gets terribly uptight about processes. Sometimes processes are important, but by and large I don't mind an unpolished process if it delivers results. I don't like hierarchies. I don't like status. I won't do it. I don't like people who impose it on others. I do want to hear what people are saying. I try to be approachable.' Those are the kind of messages you can get across very powerfully.

So if the post had been for an organization for whom hierarchy is very important, you probably wouldn't have applied or been appointed in the first place?

Possibly. So why did I go for the civil service? Good question, really. I suppose I thought I could change that. I think in the places I have worked I did have an impact, people were kind enough to say so, but I think the rest of the civil service is far too hierarchical and status-conscious. So I think you have got to make a judgment: 'Do I think I can change it?' I was younger then, and I was more arrogant and thought I could do it, but after 11 or 12 years of it I thought it was probably time to move on and let someone else have a go.

You were talking earlier about how the first six months in an organization are often the most difficult for a leader, but also the ones with the greatest opportunity. Is it the failure to recognize this that causes certain leaders to be successful in one organization, and to fail in the next?

Yes, I think it is one of the problems, particularly for people going from the public sector to the private or vice versa.

The culture change is too much?

Yes, I think that is one of the reasons why someone coming in, who does try to transplant a style which has grown up in a different sector or a different kind of organization, will find it very difficult. I think you have just got to try to be good in picking out what really matters to an organization.

Respect, trust and shared values

Throughout the course of the six interviews, I had heard time and again about the importance of being yourself. Sir Michael Bichard had talked about the importance of sharing the organization's values, and about where those values came from. I wanted to establish conclusively that the values that my other subjects talked about, such as honesty and integrity, were actually inherent in his personality.

You were saying earlier that you are not hierarchical in any way. As a leader, is your self-image important? I don't mean image as in brand, I am talking about image in terms of how people perceive you, how people see you.

Well I am certainly trying to portray, or convey, an image which is real. This is not an image which is fabricated. I am trying to convey who I am to people. I think that's really, really important. The one thing that no leader can do without is trust. People need to feel that they know what you stand for, where you stand, and that is about the image, but image is sometimes used only in terms of something which is fabricated. I am talking about conveying what you are.

A lot of people have said to me, 'I didn't always agree with you, but I never lost respect for you. I always knew where I was with you. I trusted you. You were honest and you had integrity'. The fact that someone doesn't agree with you is second order, actually, because you never always agree with someone. The question is, can you walk away from a disagreement with a shared respect?

For example, people used to come into the departmental management meetings, and sometimes they would be shocked by the kind of passionate debate and the arguments that took place. The great thing about that team was that they didn't shy away from conflict around an issue. If there were disagreements, they disagreed, and they were able to walk away from that issue and that debate with the team intact, because it was such a passionate team which wanted to improve the quality of education, or wanted to get people back into work. And that's why there was passion. And that's fantastic. You are not scoring points off each other. You are not trying to do someone down for the sake of doing them down. You try to have an honest, grown-up debate about how you improve literacy in schools and there will be disagreements about that.

I think the leader's task is to try, in that setting, to create an environment where people do feel able to be passionate, without the team falling apart. For example, I tend to use humour quite a lot as a way of maintaining the right balance in a team. I try to use humour in a way that I think will diffuse situations, particularly when a discussion is getting a bit out of hand, or getting a bit personal. It's important that the team know each other well enough. I have spent a lot of time with teams developing their knowledge of each other and sharing the commitment of what we are trying to do. If they know each other well enough, then you can diffuse a situation with a bit of humour.

I remember in the Education Department, there was a guy whom David Blunkett didn't warm to immediately. I said to David, 'This guy's good, we must stick with him'. After about a month David took me to one side and said, 'You're right, he's the vinegar on the chips!' And that's exactly what he was on the team, and the team knew that. He didn't take it to extremes, but he was searching and was questioning, and quite challenging. And once you know that, you can cope with a lot of challenge from that person. That's the leader's task, to create this field, this stage on which people can perform and interact.

I can see how valuable humour might be, even just to diffuse situations. To a prospective leader, what other tips would you offer for creating and maintaining the balance of a good team?

You do need to really understand the people you are working with, and what they are bringing to the team. People who are individual performers are sometimes brilliant. There is a point at which, however, the brilliance of their individual performance is not enough, because if you really believe that the organization benefits from a strong team, and you have someone who just cannot be a member of that team, then I'm afraid you've just got to recognize that it's not working, and that it's not going to work.

Leaders tend not to realize that the organization is watching. The organization takes note of what is happening. If someone just cocks a snook at the rest of the team, bad-mouths them behind their back and think they will get away with it, then the rest of the organization thinks that's the way in which you get to the top. I think promotion decisions in an organization are some of the most important that a leader takes. Because people really care about their careers, and they are watching what you do when you fill posts.

In the Department, because the civil service had been dominated with the ethos that policy mattered more than delivery and management, we made a conscious effort to recruit a mix of skills. After two or three years, when we advertised for senior posts, we said that we would give preference to people who had a mix of policy and operational skills. So people who hadn't taken the opportunity to develop their operational skills were at a disadvantage, and they began to realize that we were serious. Until then, people had said that operational management was important, but had gone on promoting people who were just policy wonks.

It's the same for an organization that says it cares about customers, but then carries on promoting people who treat customers with disdain. The organization is watching, and reckons that customers really aren't that important. We talked about vision and values earlier, but vision and values have got to affect the way the organization works, and what the organization does. So if you say that customer service is important, you have to appraise people on the contribution they make to improve customer service. If you don't, then people reckon that customer service isn't important. And if you are training people, are you putting your training budget into improving customer service skills?

I spent a lot of time in the Education Department on creativity. We all talk about creativity, but there are ways in which you can help people to develop creative skills. So are you putting your training budget into that, or are you carrying on spending it on time management, and first-aid? So you have to have your vision in front of you. You have got to be constantly scanning what is happening in the organization and question whether all of your systems are supporting that vision. Very often they are not, and the leader is in the position, more than anyone else, to do something about it. Ask yourself whether the things that make the organization tick actually reflect the vision and the values. If they don't, then you have got to adjust it. Recruitment is obviously key. Are you recruiting the people who will have the attitudes and values that we say we want?

I get the impression that the Benefits Agency, and the Department of Education and Employment, were organizations which required formal recruitment procedures, induction procedures, appraisal procedures. But I sense that you would have preferred not to have those formal procedures in place?

No, I don't think that's right. I think I spent most of my time trying to simplify the procedures, which doesn't mean you don't have them at all. For example, I'm passionate about equality, and in order to ensure that you are recruiting in a way that delivers equality you have got to have procedures. I understand that. If you are going to have business planning, for instance, you have got to have some kind of framework, people have got to produce business plans. But I think the trick in the public sector is to try to minimize all of that bureaucracy. It does get in the way. I have seen appraisal systems which were sophisticated and intellectually defensible which got in the way of improving the organization's performance. That is not acceptable.

The odd thing is that when you produce something like a business planning process, everyone wants to impress, and they start producing huge amounts of paper. At the university, I find that I have to tell people that I don't want lots of paper. For most issues, what I want is six sides, no more, and I want honesty about whether or not we are achieving our priorities and what the problems and issues are. Then we can have a debate around that, so it's vital not to obfuscate those issues with huge amounts of paper.

Stress and pressure

I was aware from the moment I had been introduced to Sir Michael Bichard that he seemed a very calm and relaxed person. It is my personal view that successful leaders are able to manage their stress effectively, and I wanted to find out Sir Michael's view. Running the Benefits Agency, surely, must have been a stressful occupation?

We talked earlier about your own personal values. You come across as someone who is calm, and who manages their stress very well. Is stress an issue for you? How do you make sure that your stress doesn't impact on your team leaders, and ultimately on the rest of the team?

I do experience stress. I suppose my stress concerns whether or not I have the time that I need to give to the different organizations that I am involved in. I find that quite difficult at times. Like everyone else, I get tired. I am not as young as I was, and I am probably working longer hours than I have ever worked.

Putting that aside, I think that whether or not you are stressed depends on what you can cope with, and what you can cope with depends upon what you have been exposed to. I had a conversation once with David Puttnam, who is a friend and worked with us in the Department. We both feel that the most effective leaders are people who, as he put it, have been through the fire. When David was chair of MGM it was a hellish time, but he came out of it stronger. He knew himself better. It is a bit like training, isn't it? The more you train the more you can cope with.

I was Chief Executive of Brent Council for six years in the early 1980s when London labour politics were absolute hell. Brent was a hung council. It was probably the most difficult organization to lead that you could imagine. People kept telling me that it's good experience, and I used to think, good experience for what? But it *was* good experience. It taught me a hell of a lot about politics. It taught me a hell of a lot about how you inspire people in the most difficult circumstances. People didn't understand what was going on. They didn't understand why the council was taking certain decisions, or why they were meeting every night until four in the morning, and changing their minds on a regular basis. And you are trying to juggle all of these things. But you come out of it a bit calmer and a bit more capable of dealing with issues. So when I went to the civil service, some of the issues that I faced were not actually that much different from Brent! So the more fire you have been through, the better equipped you are to deal with the stress and the pressure.

I see leadership as a journey, and you need to be thinking about what you are learning, and whether you are putting yourself in a position to learn. Now you may not want to put yourself into a Brent Council or an MGM, but at the other end of the scale I have seen people who carefully nurture their career so that they never lead in difficult situations. I don't want them around me because I will make mistakes, we all make mistakes, and the organization will go through difficult times. I want people who have actually dug themselves or their organization out of a hole.

In the civil service, I knew a brilliant young policy guy, who actually went out and ran the Harlesden Benefit Office. Now that is a bloody difficult management job. But he realized that he had been to university, he had come into the Department as a policy adviser, and yet he knew nothing about managing people on a day-to-day basis, or having to take decisions quickly without having all the information in front of him. In the Harlesden Benefit Office, someone's livelihood depends on that decision, and that brings its own pressure. And this guy came back a much better leader, much better equipped to cope with hard situations. I want people who can cope with the crises without going into freefall.

I still maintain that I learned most in my career from the eight months I spent managing an Aldi supermarket in the Midlands.

Absolutely. My daughter, who is 22 and did a degree in leisure and tourism, spent a year as duty manager at the leisure centre off the Edgware Road in London: crap building, huge staff turnover, some of who didn't speak English, a clientele many of who didn't speak English, equipment and resources that constantly broke down. And I was full of admiration because actually I would have found that a stretch. But she put herself in that situation and some people do that, and as a result, by the time they are 35 or 40, maybe younger, then they are pretty well the finished article. But there are others, in their 40s and 50s, whom I wouldn't want around me when the shit hits the fan.

If you're running a national organization, and you find yourself on the front page of *The Guardian*, you've still got to keep calm under those sorts of pressures because if you don't keep calm, then you make bad decisions. And you have got to have sufficient confidence in your decision-making to make the decision that you think is right. Sometimes, you are faced with decisions where, whatever you do, you will be criticized.

For example, when I was in Brent I sacked three social workers at the end of one of the first major child abuse cases, the Jasmine Beckford case. The press and the media wanted them sacked. The council were ambivalent. Obviously, the social workers didn't want them sacked. In the end you have to go into a room and ask yourself what is the right thing to do? Forget about what everyone is telling you, and forget about the flack you are going to get. Once you have done that once or twice you feel much better equipped to take the hard decisions. Of course you ask people's opinions. You get as much information as you can in the time you've got. But you can't defend decisions you don't believe in, so you have got to take decisions that you believe in. You have got to have the confidence to do it, and be prepared to take the flack.

Presumably the emotions you have just described came to the fore during the Soham Murder Inquiry?

Quite. Yes. It's an odd thing to say, but I was lucky in the sense that what I'd done before equipped me very well to deal with the Soham Inquiry. I knew the cultures of the organizations. I had been a clerk to a police authority. I had been a solicitor. I had worked for public services. I knew the constraints under which they were working. I also had been at the receiving end of an inquiry at Brent, because the inquiry into the death of Jasmine Beckford was national news for about six months. I knew that inquiries are really bruising, damaging encounters, and that you need to get them over with as quickly as possible. The police of Humberside needed it sorted so that they could move on and continue to provide a service. So you bring all that to bear, but you can bring it to bear only if you have actually thought about those things. I think some people I observe don't reflect sufficiently. They don't reflect on what makes for a successful encounter, and what makes for an unsuccessful encounter. It's particularly important, at the end of a good day, to go home and think about why the day has gone well.

I love watching other leaders. As you probably gather, I am a great friend of David Blunkett and we worked very closely together. I have always watched David, and learned a lot from him. Sometimes it's worth thinking through why another leader took the decision that they did: what information did they use, and was it a good decision? I do that all the time with other people. I have always done that. People don't reflect enough on what works and what doesn't work, and why other people are successful, and how they make successful decisions.

Do you consciously take time out to reflect, or does it just happen?

I don't take time out, in the sense that I don't take sabbaticals. I have always involved myself in working with people and other organizations on leadership and management development activities. I talk a lot to groups of younger managers and leaders. I find that a good way to learn myself, because they challenge you. If I go and talk to a group of hungry young managers, I know that they'll want to take me apart, they'll want to challenge me, they'll want to find where I am missing something, where there are contradictions in what I have to say. That's a learning experience.

I chair the Legal Services Commission, and found it fascinating to look at how that has been led and managed, and what comparisons are to be made with the university, and what one can learn from the other. Maybe it is easier to do it if you go away for a month to the Himalayas to reflect, but I believe that I now reflect almost naturally.

Right, but if you have an immediate challenge, do you have the equivalent of going off for a ten-minute walk? Is that process in itself calming? Is it solution-providing?

Yes, I think there are some decisions that you have got to take where you do need to take a bit of time out to go and think about it, and be pretty methodical. Not everyone would do this. Some people can rely on gut instinct, possibly. But I would fairly methodically try to balance the advantages and disadvantages, the costs and benefits and try to make the best, the most rational, decision. Although in some situations you have to factor other things in, because rationality is not on its own enough. Again, that's all about gaining experience from different situations.

We talked about stress in terms of remaining calm. I have always associated stress with inhibiting energy and creativity, and we have talked a lot about how important those two things are to a leader. Are you aware that stress is actually sapping your energy or sapping that passion, and if so, what do you do about it? Do you have something that snaps you out of it?

I don't know about that. I am not often aware of feeling under great stress except, as I say, trying to take too many things on.

So in that sense it is about managing ourselves better – and having an unbelievably good secretary! That is not a cliché or an off-hand remark. Some of the worst times in my career have been having private offices or secretaries who weren't in tune with me. At times they almost deliberately seemed to make life more difficult. The best times in my life have been in the civil service where I had a private secretary, and a diary secretary, who were absolutely in tune. I remember that David Blunkett would be pretty ruthless about someone who came in and just didn't fit.

So my stress is about activity and time and it's about having someone who can minimize that for me in a way. Otherwise, I actually think you need a certain level of stress and adrenaline in order to stretch yourself and stretch the organization, and I couldn't thrive in a place where there was none of that. Some people might accuse me of taking on some of these other roles because there isn't enough stress and adrenaline in 'just' running a university. That is probably a bit harsh.

Do you find it easy or difficult to say no? Is part of the reason that you have so much on your plate because you don't say no?

I can say no. But I find it very difficult to say no to people I owe. I mean, for example, people who have worked for me and have done a good job and have supported me. Then I find it very difficult to decline to come and do a speech for them, or something like that. The issue with speeches is that you have got to write them yourself. I was talking to Herbert Lamming recently – Lord Lamming – who has done a number of inquiries, and he was saying that one has to set standards. If I am invited to speak somewhere, then it has got to be good, and so you have got to prepare it properly. I cannot cope with people who go to a conference with two or three hundred people and they haven't prepared, because they are wasting two or three hundred hours of time there. So you have got to maintain your standards, and that means sometimes doing things like speeches for people who you owe one to.

Otherwise I'm OK saying no most of the time. I now have more excuses for saying no, because I just can't fit things in. I mean, I would take a lot of persuading to take on another inquiry like Soham, for example, because I just don't think I could cope with it with all the other things I am doing at the moment. I hadn't realized how exhausting something like that can be.

When you were asked to chair the Soham Murder Inquiry, what was your initial thought?

Well I had promised David Blunkett that if there was something he wanted me to do which was important, I would do it. So I thought it was important enough to do, really. But I now have great respect for people who chair those sorts of inquiries because it does take it out of you. I was down in my office in Holborn every weekend, and during the week. I did this job in the morning and evening and that was a killer really!

People often think that one mistake that leaders make is that they want to be liked, they want to be adored.

Has that ever been an issue for you? Do you not care?

I would rather be liked than not liked, but I don't think that's the standard you should set or measure. The standard is whether or not people trust and respect you, I think, because sometimes the conclusion you come to is that you are going to have to do some things that people won't like. You don't need to do them in a way that is unnecessarily aggressive or unpleasant, and you need to show that you understand that these things are difficult.

If there was a difficult decision that people weren't going to like, I would always try to say, 'I know you are not going to like this. I am really sorry. I have thought this one through, I have listened to what you have had to say, but I just think this is what we need to do, and I am just asking you to do it as best we can'. And I find that, by and large, people do that. So I don't curry favour. Some people don't like me, others do like me. I'm a bit abrasive sometimes, I'm a bit brusque and a bit sharp to people. But that's because I am passionate about what I do.

Small and large organizations

Earlier we talked about the challenges faced when a leader moves between the public and private sectors, or vice versa. What about leaders who move from large, corporate organizations to small ones? If you were persuaded to go and lead a team of six people, what would you do differently? Are all the skills you have described transferable to a small organization?

I have done it twice in the last five years, actually. I chaired one start-up company, and another near start-up company. I think the answer is that a lot of the skills are applicable, because again they are about people and clients. I think you learn a lot from different situations. I mean, I chair this consultancy company, they were all about 29 years old, and amazingly bright, really up for it. I feel a bit like the great-grand-daddy of the organization! But that has taught me something about clients which you don't get from really big public sector organizations, in the sense that if we don't keep our clients we don't survive. So you really value your clients and you want to learn what it is that they want from you and how you can get their return business.

But that's a value, surely?

Yes, that is right. But it applies the same client focus which I have always taken very seriously, but it is doing it on a smaller scale. I think that is good for you – it is all about the learning experience. I know it's a cliché, but once you stop learning, you are not much use to anyone. I found a quote from Michelangelo, when he was 87, and he said then, 'I am still learning'. That is how people stay fresh, I think. That's why, when I was in the Department, I was so passionate about learning for older people, because I think if older people keep on learning, and are involved in some form of learning, then their independence will continue, their curiosity in the proper sense of the word will continue, they will stay younger. I think it's the same for leaders and managers. You have got to be constantly learning and taking advantages of the opportunities of going into different situations.

I haven't done a lot of private sector work in my career. I have been a non-exec, and I have chaired these two companies. I have led two local authorities, in Brent and Gloucestershire, the Next Step agency, two government departments, a university, and the Legal Services Commission. If someone asked me what

I was proud of, it's the fact that I have been able to shift myself across what were quite different organizations, and apply my skills in different settings.

It sounds as if you are writing your epitaph?

Well I do think that leaders ought to be aware of the time to go, to move on. I believe that it's the role of the leader to think about succession planning. One reason I left the Department of Education was because I thought there were some really great people who could take my job, and I was delighted that one of them did and I had a hand in that. And several others have gone off to do permanent secretary and chief executive roles elsewhere. That's great. I began to feel uncomfortable, because I could see that I was in their way. I just thought it was the time to get out really. So you need to know when to move on.

I have been itching to ask this. Earlier, you described leadership as a journey. Where are you on this journey?

I personally am at the stage where I don't think I want to be a chief executive in the future. I have been a chief executive now for 26 years. That's unusual. The thing about being a chief executive is that you are the one who is always at the end of the line in accountability. I have got to the stage where I think I have had enough of that really. I think I could apply and use my skills in better ways as a chairman or in some other role. I know it sounds again like a cliché, but I don't want to be working six days a week any more, to be honest.

So when you are no longer a chief executive, what will provide the passion and the energy?

Well I would like to have a couple of chairman roles, probably in the public sector because I don't have the experience in the private sector. But I will write, I will speak, I edit things, and I will carry on doing that. I can't imagine that I am just going to disappear, but I will certainly not have the same high profile. I mean, I have turned down an awful lot of interesting things because I just haven't got time to fit them in.

The self-critic

I really thought I had established the key principles of leading people in my discussion with Sir Michael Bichard. I was building a picture of someone with vision, with integrity, and with sympathy and respect for their own values, and those of their organization. This person gives their people real ownership of the vision, and places strong people to lead their key departments and teams. They are passionate about what they do, they communicate well, they listen, and they attempt to break down some of the obstacles that stand in the way of their people performing well. The more fire they have experienced, the better they are able to handle the stress and pressure associated with leading teams.

But Sir Michael clearly had more to say, and nothing had prepared me for what was to come.

Overall, would you say that you are a good leader?

I am incredibly self-critical. We haven't talked about that. I think the best leaders are incredibly self-critical, actually. People who know me know that one of the things I do as well as anyone is to listen. If you are a big guy with a deep voice who is fairly robust, people sometimes misunderstand that and they don't realize that you are all the time listening and picking up signals. I think I am pretty good at that. People don't spot it. I don't miss anything much. And I also think that if you are big and ugly and male, with a deep voice, people think that you are not necessarily very self-critical, and I am hugely self-critical.

So do I think I am a good leader? I do as good a job as anyone else could do in most of the situations that I have been in. So in that sense I am an arrogant leader, and yes I think I can do it as well as anyone. Do I do it well enough? Never really, because you have got to keep learning.

What form does the self-criticism take? Wishing you had done some things differently?

Oh yes. Am I going to give you examples of it?

You don't have to!

Yes, of course I think I could have done some things differently. I could have handled certain people differently, yes. I could have handled situations differently. In terms of the succession planning and team-building here, it hasn't quite worked out as planned, which is why I am staying another two years, because I want to try to leave it in a good state. The university is doing really well. But I'm not quite satisfied … I am not satisfied yet. I think I have got to grips with management and leadership in the organization, and have got a really good programme going now, which has had a real impact. It has been terribly well received by the 20 or 30 people who have got on the programme, and I can see, for the first time, a real interest in management. We should have started that about two years ago. It just didn't come together quickly enough. So of course there are things you could have done better.

For a lot of people, the fact that they could have done something better would gnaw away at them. Are you someone who can make the decision, accept you have done it wrong, and move on? Is that a sign of a good leader? Or perhaps it gnaws away at you too?

It does gnaw away at me really. That is why I was just pausing. I don't take mistakes well. But I think that I do have the ability to draw a line under it at the end of the day, because otherwise it destroys you and the organization. I mean, there comes a point when you can't do much about it. You have got to learn from it. There are probably painful lessons about how you handled people or situations. If you let it destroy your confidence, then you are not going to lead. Leaders have got to have confidence.

And you are a confident person?

I am a confident person, but if that confidence spills over into arrogance then you are not a good leader.

Are you aware, in your own approach, when the definitions of confidence and arrogance become blurred?

I think I am so obsessive about *not* being arrogant that I have stopped short well before I say something and I think 'Christ, that sounds arrogant'. If I do, I am normally able to say, 'Sorry, I didn't mean to put it quite like that'.

Yes, I hate arrogance. And once you are arrogant you don't listen. That's the issue. You are so bloody cock sure, why should you listen? No one has got anything to offer you, have they? There is nothing you can learn, because you know it all! One of the problems of becoming a permanent secretary is that suddenly everyone thinks you know everything! And whereas you may be used to developing the kind of climate we were talking about earlier, where I want challenge, and foster engagement and discussion and creativity, they were just waiting there for your word. That's terrifying. That's why I need a challenging private office of staff around me. I had a fantastic private office in both the Benefits Agency and the Department of Education. You need people who can just come in and give you the bad news and the feedback that you don't necessarily want to hear.

For example, the guy who ran my private office in the Benefits Agency, Terry, is a very close friend, and is now the chief executive of a large government agency. He's just a brilliant, brilliant guy. After a while, I guess it must have been about nine months, he would come through the door and say, 'Boss, I think you should know that ...'. I remember we were going through a particularly bad time, introducing the disability allowance, which was a disaster. We had inherited it, and it had just ended up with not paying people who were terminally ill. The journalist Esther Rantzen was trying to run programmes about it, and we were running around trying to pay people before, sometimes literally, they died. After about nine months of this, I said to Terry, 'If you come through that bloody door once more and say "Boss, I think you should know that ..." I am going to kill you!'

But both he and the other people we had around us would come in and sit down and would be able to say, 'I don't think you handled that very well', or 'They are not getting the message you know', and that's vital.

Some leaders just cut themselves off. They just want to be reassured, but they don't have someone around them who can be honest with them. I don't want someone who is going to keep telling me that it is all doom and gloom, but I do want someone who is sensitive to you in the way that you have got to be sensitive to other people. That person needs to know when there is a time to give you the bit of bad news, and when actually you just need a bit of support. If you've just been on national television, and you've been asked when you are going to resign, then it's not the time to say that the unit down the road are not very happy about something. It will wait!

Inspiration

You have given me one very good example earlier, but who do you take inspiration from? Who are the leaders out there that you think tick all the boxes?

I think the people I respect most are the people who have done the job for a long time and who have consistently delivered.

I think some leaders are a bit fly-by-night really – they move here, there and everywhere and you are never quite sure whether they did actually deliver lasting change anywhere. The public sector is particularly prone to people who play around with the structures and then go before they have changed the behaviour, and you are never quite sure whether the organization is better or worse for their having been there.

The people I respect are the people who have employed a combination of all the things I have talked about. I have mentioned David Puttnam, whom I worked with at the Department. He is someone who ticks all the boxes for me. He is great in terms of the impact he can have with people, across all ages. He can make contact with people at all sorts of different levels, he is full of ideas and creativity, and he is a real human being who cares about people.

Dennis Stevenson, who is our chancellor here at the university, is very stimulating, and also someone who has a wide range of experience. He's run Pearson, he's run the Halifax, he's run his own business. He's a strong supporter of the arts and a number of voluntary groups and organizations – I think he is great.

I don't know him, but I admire greatly Terry Leahy, CEO of Tesco, because I think he has done really well over a period of time. I admire success too. Over the last 12 months I have got to know Philip Green. You can't deny, he is an inspiration. To go into his office and see him with a group of young designers, and the way in which he still somehow manages to stay in tune with a younger generation, it's amazing really.

Change

Is leadership becoming more difficult?

Yes, I think it is getting more difficult. I think it's because the environment is changing so quickly. As a leader, you have to be keeping a close watch on what is going on out there that affects your organization. What is going to happen in ten years' time to a university that currently stays afloat because 37 of our students are from overseas? What happens when India and China start having universities that have got the kind of reputation that our universities have got at the moment?

Leading people is changing because people are becoming more challenging – their expectations are higher, they expect more from their organization, and clients expect more from their organization. For example, I have noticed in five years here that what the students expect has changed and developed. They are actually paying for their education now – they are clients, and they want good services. Our website is not good enough for them. And they're right, it's not good enough! We are just doing two floors of work downstairs, because we looked like a second-rate technical college really. We weren't providing students with access to learning at weekends and, again, it just wasn't good enough. The reception area wasn't good enough, so we put money into doing that this summer. So I think the pressures are always pretty substantial in any organization.

I sometimes say to audiences that every leader likes to think that this is the most challenging time there has ever been in the world, because it makes you feel good. Well actually there may be reasons for the current challenges, and IT must be a large part of that. IT and technology have contributed to changing expectations. A couple of weeks ago, I spoke to the Annual Conference of Forensic Scientists. They wanted me to talk about quality, and I was saying that one of the issues about quality is that it's not static. Quality is about what people expect you to deliver and from the view of the forensic scientists, DNA, for example, has changed dramatically what people expect from that profession over the last ten years. If you look at the police and the Soham inquiry, ten years ago people wouldn't have even thought it was reasonable to expect that police forces could and should exchange information. Now they expect it, and the police aren't delivering it, and so they are not yet providing quality, in my view. So technology is changing everything all of the time.

Take customer service as another example. Five years ago, an enquiry would come in by letter, and the sender would expect a seven-day response. Then fax arrived, and they would expect a same-day response. Now with email – 15 or 20 minutes is the expectation!

I don't think people should accept bad customer service from the university. Our customer service is still not good enough. We are not sufficiently consumer-focused, and part of that is because academics can be introspective. So part of my job is to try to deal with that, and to try and get everyone to understand that the most successful universities in ten years' time are probably going to be the universities that provide the best service to their students, and their graduates, and that's one of the things we have done a lot of here. We have worked much more to help our graduates when they leave to get jobs in business. I want our students to tell other people that at this university they care about you from the time you make your first contact right the way through your career.

That's a dramatic difference. What's the point of us training fashion designers and then watching most of them fail? So we now have the Centre for Fashion Enterprise, where we are taking a dozen graduates and helping them through their first two collections, giving them business advice, investing with them, taking a share in the company. It's only a small share – 10 per cent – but I found out yesterday that one of these companies, after three years, is worth six million quid!

So it is all about adapting to the changing world and changing expectations.

Innate or learned?

Are all the leadership skills we have talked about something you can learn? You are not born a leader?

Well you can learn them, yes, absolutely. I said earlier that people have different styles, and they need to find a way of being a leader in their own style. I'm probably brasher than some, but I respect quiet leaders because they probably find it easier to get people to talk to them. As I said earlier, it takes you a long time to get through the barrier of being six-foot-two and big. That is a serious issue sometimes, particularly when you are trying to develop relationships with women who are working in the organization. I have changed my style quite a lot in 20 years. I'm not saying I have changed a lot in the last few years, because I think when I went to Lambeth and then Brent they just transformed my understanding of the issues of equality and racism, so that changed my life really. But early in my career I was certainly one of the lads and fairly brash.

I think it's important to restate that the leadership journey is about learning. I'm more confident as a leader, since I left the civil service I suppose. I think one of the most important things is people's confidence in you. You should remember that. Remember how leaders treated you. The most important role model for me was my very first chief executive at Reading because I was pretty unpolished. I was from a very working-class family and he really taught me how to behave, and he also gave me space, which I try to do with younger people too now. Back then I was too aggressive, too brash, and not someone you would want to know. But he still gave me the space. He would sit there and smile and just watch me sometimes get it wrong. He's a hero. He died a long time ago now, but he's a hero, and I try to do the same with young staff myself.

My other big influence was David Blunkett. I'd been in the civil service running the Benefits Agency for five or six years, had been Permanent Secretary for a year, but I suppose I always felt that I was an outsider, and I wasn't totally confident in that environment. Then Blunkett just came along and said, 'I've got very high standards, but you are bloody good and you and I can do great things and we are going to do great things'. And suddenly you think, 'Right, OK, I can do this!'

Do you play that conversation in your mind at times when you need a bit of an energy boost?

I think the fact that people have invested their confidence in you, if you really respect them, makes a difference to you. That's something that leaders shouldn't forget. Some leaders are so important they forget that a word from them stays with people forever.

I get really quite moved sometimes when I do these speaking engagements. This is not meant to sound self-serving, but sometimes people come up to me and say, 'You changed my life!' And I think 'Bloody hell – was it for the better?' And they remind you of a conversation which might not have figured in your life but made a huge impact on them. That's why, when you go out, you have got to be aware that you are sending messages all the time, and the best leaders know they are sending messages. They are not inhibited. Some leaders get so nervous that what they do will be misinterpreted, that they don't do anything. They are scared stiff that they will be misinterpreted and that's a tragedy really, because actually leadership can be fun, but if you're like that it's never going to be fun.

But the answer to your question is, I suppose, from the time I started working with Blunkett, which is now ten years ago, I felt confident about me as a leader. And then when you begin to reflect that you have been doing it for 26 years, you realize it hasn't been a total disaster.

It has been a huge pleasure to meet you.

I would think it's been as boring as hell.

That's the self-critic in you again!

Conclusions and recommendations

Sir Michael Bichard is an enigma. Here is a man with decades of experience of leading prominent, public sector teams, and then promoted to the highest ranks of the civil service. A man who, at the Benefits Agency, led a team of 65,000. Yet also a man who acknowledges his own self-criticism, and who all but apologized that his views on leading teams would make 'boring as hell' reading. Coming from some, this may sound or read like false modesty. But there's the enigma. Sir Michael Bichard is nothing but straight-talking, unfussy, sincere and, above all, natural. It would be hard to meet someone less prone to false modesty than him.

Despite the self-criticism, Sir Michael is charged with energy and passion for what he does. Passion is not something you can imitate, so he would advise any aspiring leader to tread a path to what they believe in or are passionate about. If you are not passionate about your organization, your people will know. It's as simple as that. Think of leading people not in terms of motivation, but in terms of the energy that you can create in them. It's the role of a good leader to remove some of the obstacles that inhibit energy, as well as to face head-on the disagreements or issues that you might prefer to ignore.

Sir Michael talks about leading teams in terms of providing a sense of purpose and direction. This may sound like management theory, until you appreciate that he has a very specific formula that he has employed throughout his career to achieve it. Share your business vision with your people, and let them really 'own' it. Then identify and share a set of values that best represents what your organization does, and how it does it. Leading people effectively is about vision, values and ownership. You might want to jot that down!

Respect is essential to a leader of people, and it's more straightforward than you might imagine to earn it. You 'be yourself'. If you make every attempt to convey to people what sort of person you are, then you will foster the trust and respect that every effective leader needs. Sir Michael's approach here might be summarized as being 'consistent but flexible'.

I was keen to establish the role that stress and pressure played in Sir Michael's career. I have long been of the opinion that successful leaders are people who have learned to manage their stress effectively. I was surprised by what I discovered. Sir Michael appears to thrive on pressure, and rates the people around him in terms of the fires they have been through. The more stress you have faced, the better able you are to handle it. I dare say that leading Brent Council throughout the 1980s makes most challenges seem fairly tame. Whilst Sir Michael is not suggesting that we should all throw ourselves into stressful situations with relish, he does suggest that those who have done so will make better people leaders.

Sir Michael Bichard is a hugely impressive man. Someone who has earned the respect and trust of his people throughout his career, using methods that are so simple to write down, yet so challenging to put into practice. He has a history of taking on rudderless or crisis-ridden organizations, and instilling them with a real sense of purpose and direction. He says that he is looking forward to a future filled with 'a couple of chairman roles' in his semi-retirement. Perhaps you should draft him a letter sooner rather than later?

Leading people checklist

If you lead a team of people yourself, here are some issues to think about. You might want to find a few, valuable minutes to take a clean sheet of paper and jot down any ideas that the following list generates.

Vision, values and ownership

Do you consciously try to create a sense of purpose and direction in your organization? Does your team feel a sense of ownership for a clear business vision? Do you have a clear set of values? Does your team share your set of values? Perhaps it's time to take a fundamental look at your organization's vision, as well as the values that you and your organization stand for. What steps can you take to give your people genuine ownership of the vision and vales?

Be yourself

Is your role as leader an act, or are you yourself? Do your own values match up to those of your organization? Do your people always know what you stand for? If not, think about whether it's appropriate for you to continue in your role in the long term. Perhaps it's time to find an organization whose values match yours more closely?

Passion

Are you passionate about what you do? Do you create and enhance energy in your organization and your people? Do you foster and encourage creativity from your people? Have you got the best team that you can around you? Is there any specific action you can take?

Communication
How well do you communicate with your people? What different communication strategies do you adopt? Could you communicate better? Do you really listen to what your people are telling you? Are you consistent, without following a dogma rigidly? Are there any obstacles that stand in your people's way that you could address right now? What action can you take?

Stress and pressure
How well do you handle stress and pressure in your role? How much fire have you had to handle in your career so far?

The self-critic
Are you a self-critic? Do you agree that being a self-critic is an important aspect of the model leader of people? What mistakes have you made? What could you have done better? What lessons have you learned from your mistakes?

The journey
Where are you on your leadership journey? What opportunities do you have for learning?

02

Sir John Tusa on managing change

Sir John Tusa, Managing Director of the Barbican Arts Centre in London

'Don't think that you can put up with people. If you can't work with them, and I mean really can't work with them, do not hang around ... Once you know that, you have simply got to move on.'

Sir John Tusa is a British television journalist and manager of arts and broadcasting organizations. Having presented Newsnight on the BBC from its inception in 1980 until 1986, he went on to become Managing Director of the BBC World Service (1986–1993).

Since retiring from his BBC World Service post, he has been critical of some BBC policies. He deprecated the former director general John Birt's focus and management style and has been outspoken about subsequent decisions to pare down World Service activities in Europe.

Since 1995 he has been Managing Director of the Barbican Arts Centre in the City of London. He is also Chairman of the Board of the Wigmore Hall in London.

He is the author of several books, including two written jointly with his wife Ann Tusa: *The Nuremberg Trial* (1983) and *The Berlin Blockade* (1988). John Tusa's most recent book is *Engaged with the Arts: Writings from the Front Line*.

He was educated at St Faith's School, Cambridge, and at Gresham's School, Holt and then at Trinity College, Cambridge, before joining the BBC as a trainee in 1960. He was awarded a knighthood in the Queen's Birthday Honours list in June 2003.

At the time I had arranged to meet Sir John Tusa, the Barbican had been the subject of a lot of press attention. It was about to celebrate its twenty-fifth birthday, and is also nearing the end of a spectacular £30 million refit. In fact, the future of the Barbican looks rosy, with an ever more diverse arts programme, now managed and co-ordinated centrally.

It hasn't always been like this. Ten years ago the Barbican was in crisis. The Royal Shakespeare Company moved out, staff morale was as low as it could be, and as a venue, the Barbican had been described as 'universally unloved'. Whoever was recruited to take over as managing director, the principal objective would be simply to survive.

The man they chose for the job was John Tusa, a BBC news journalist, author and former Managing Director of the BBC World Service. Together with his Artistic Director, Graham Sheffield, he has transformed the Barbican into the thriving and diverse arts complex that it is today.

I could see straightaway why he would make a great subject for a chapter of a book about managing change. First of all, though, I was keen to learn about why he had taken the role on. What sort of person relishes the challenge of rejuvenating a universally unloved arts complex? What qualities did he think would be required? I wondered whether he had appreciated the extent of the challenge he took on?

Change is a fact of life, and in business we are all called upon either to manage or to endure substantial and sustained organizational change. Every week, another commentator argues that the organizations that will thrive in the next decade are the ones who continually adapt their offering in line with a constantly changing marketplace. If we are to thrive as managers, we need to harness the skills required to manage change effectively. Who better to offer us advice but Sir John Tusa?

The pace of change

I began my discussion with Sir John Tusa by referring to a quotation from the Chartered Management Institute. It read:

> *'It is widely accepted that the pace of change has intensified in recent years. The impact this has had on the organisational landscape in the UK has been matched only by the effect on individuals.'*

I asked Sir John if he agreed that the pace of change had intensified, and about the impact of change.

Yes, I suppose it has. Why do I sound slightly cautious about it? I think as far as the arts are concerned, theatre is theatre, music is music, classical music is classical music. On the other hand, when you look at what we were doing in the concert hall ten years ago, it was by and large the orchestra and nothing else. And yet within the last ten years the use of combination art forms, such as orchestra with video, is now far more accepted. It is not every orchestra, nor every concert, but it is much more common. So the sorts of things that go into concerts have changed. For example, we have just had a Steve Reich Festival. I wouldn't say that would have been unthinkable ten years ago, but it would have been highly unlikely. And that was almost all multi-form. He has written two operas accompanied by DVDs with video clips. That is certainly a change that has occurred in the last ten years.

And so what you are staging has changed over the last ten years?

Yes, and the way in which artists express themselves has changed. Now artists use the orchestra, they use electronics, sampling, video and live movement. This has developed over the last ten years, there is no question about that.

What has caused the change? Is it a result of the technology that has been made available? Has that provided another art form to exploit, if you like, or do you think it's the changing demands of audiences? Perhaps it's both?

I think the technology has come first. Artists have got interested in it, and then developed their expertise in it. At the same time the audiences, who are also technologically aware, have followed. I think it is probably that way around, but clearly if you didn't have an audience that was also technologically sophisticated, they wouldn't turn up to experience it. On the other hand, there are lots of people who still only want a concert, who only want a play, and they don't want it messed around with. Or who just want nice drawings and paintings, who don't like video art.

But there is an increasingly significant audience which does like it. And all that has really certainly changed at an accelerating pace over the last ten years. To give you one idea of how big the change has been, ten years ago the Royal Shakespeare Company were our resident company, and that's what the Barbican was known for. It was Shakespeare. Then they left, and their audience left with them, because that was what they were interested in.

Ten years on and we have Simon McBurney and Complicite and his last show, The Elephant Vanishes. And people were queuing up the stairs to get in. It was a very difference audience. That was a production which was extremely radical in its use of things like video, film, lighting and how the production was done. So I think that the pace with which that sort of production has developed over the last ten years is very real.

Opportunities for change

A lot has been written about the Royal Shakespeare Company's decision to move out of the Barbican almost ten years ago. I couldn't help but imagine that this must have come as something of a blow to the recently recruited Managing Director. What went through Sir John Tusa's mind when he discovered that his major resident company had decided to 'part company', so to speak? How does the effective leader react to a situation like this?

Do you think that the RSC moving out of the Barbican presented an enormous opportunity for you? Did it provide a catalyst for change?

Well it was certainly a catalyst. Everybody told us that we couldn't manage. So, yes, it was a huge catalyst and an opportunity, and we certainly wouldn't be doing the sort of things that we do now, or anything like them, if the RSC were still with us. So it was a huge change and a huge opportunity.

Essentially what we have done is to realign the approach to all the arts from being 'small c classical' and 'small c conservative', to arts which are much more engaged with the newer available forms of expression. I reckon that if you were to look at our Arts Diary from ten years ago and compare it with today's, it would be absolutely unrecognisable.

Can I wind back the clock a decade or so to 1995? Back then, the Barbican was described as 'crisis-ridden' and 'universally unloved'. What made you think, from your own career perspective, that the Barbican was the right opportunity for you?

There were two things, one comparatively defensive and one not. At the time, I was working in BBC television news, and I knew I had reached an age where my shelf-life in front of the camera was very limited.

Also, reading the news was alright, but it wasn't terribly stretching, especially having led the BBC World Service for six years. So I had been vaguely keeping my eye open for an appropriate challenge. Because the Barbican is a multi art-form centre, rather than an opera house, a concert hall or an art gallery, I thought this was probably the only one that I had any authority to manage. And so when it seemed to be imploding and crisis-ridden, I thought I had very little to lose. I knew I needed to move and I was very lucky that that happened when it did.

I'd really like to know what it was like for you. You take over a crisis-ridden Barbican. Where on earth do you start? What is the process for looking at what needs to be changed, both in terms of the scale and its impact?

I don't believe that anybody who goes into an institution ever has any real idea of what the nature of the problems are. I think everybody goes in, to one degree or another, fairly ignorant, or else they are kidding themselves. I think that's probably necessary, because if you knew everything that was wrong you would probably conclude that it was too great a challenge!

I believed, and thank goodness I was right, that the basic finances were alright. The revenue budget was fine. Beyond that, once I got in and met the senior directors, I just knew immediately that the set-up I inherited was not going to work. The atmosphere – in terms of how people behaved, the sort of things they said, how they argued, and the general cultural atmosphere – was completely negative and sterile. There was also a great deal of back-biting and in-fighting.

And do you think that this attitude had created the crisis in the first place?

It had both created it, and it had been created and made worse by it. Either way, it was very, very bad. And some of the people who were reflecting or expressing this atmosphere were people who had been appointed by the previous incumbent, which was worrying. So I knew within six weeks that at least two of the senior people had to go.

As soon as that?

Oh yes. So I said to the City of London Corporation, 'I cannot work with A and B'.

And if there is some core advice I could pass on, it would be this. Don't think that you can put up with people. If you can't work with them, and I mean really can't work with them, do not hang around. Don't kid yourself that things are going to get better, or that you can do something about it. Once you know that, you have simply got to move on. And that was easily the best thing that I did.

And what effect did that have on the wider staff? I understand that morale was not at its highest at that point, anyway. So what effect did that actually have?

Well the short-term impact was that they assumed that there would be even more blood-letting. When I made the first change, I knew there was going to be a second, so that needed some careful footwork. So there was a certain assumption that heads were going to be rolling, and that was something we just had to get through. Once three months passed, and then six, people realized that it was *not* a cull of all of the senior management. But those six months were just something that we had to go through. I knew that once we had different people in that it was going to work differently. And I think that when I appointed new people, the staff understood, and could see for themselves, that these were different kinds of people. First, the new people were competent; second, the new people were open; and third, the staff could begin to sense that the atmosphere among the directors was changing for the better.

In fact, of my six directors, four of us have been together for ten years. And the remaining two have joined within the last five. So we've been very stable, and whilst you might say that stability itself has its own problems, it is a very different order of problem. But once people could see that the team was there, and that the team was open and settled, then morale started to improve.

Another change was that we started to introduce open staff meetings. Surprisingly, it had never happened before. Never. When we announced the first staff meeting, morale was such that many saw it just an attempt at a short-term fix. I remember asking somebody after the meeting what they had thought of it and they said, 'Well it's all very well, but it won't happen again, will it?' I had to assure him that it would happen three times a year. Most people were fairly dubious at first, but we did it, and we still do it. So that was also another very, very important milestone.

You mentioned earlier that people questioned whether the changes to the senior management team were part of a wider cull. I think you said that in a situation like that, you have just got to be open and honest about what is happening. Would that be right? What advice would you give a company director who knows that they have got to go through that change themselves in their organization?

Well given that I knew that there was one other person who still had to go, I had to be careful what I said when the first person came and asked if there would be any more. I had to use rather political machinations and just hope that the time between change one and change two was not so long that it would damage relations even further.

So with something like that I think there was no alternative but to be cautious and not to sound too evasive. But I think I could say quite openly, 'This is not the start of a wholesale programme'. There isn't any easy way, but above all, what you *don't* say is, 'No, no, no, that's it', when you know that something else is going to have to be changed.

About three years later there was quite a lot of further change, but that was for different reasons, because having got the directors right we then knew that the place could only be run properly with a lot of co-operation from the departmental heads. They, by and large, took the view that they had a job to do, they had a job description to fulfil, and that was what they did. So when invited to contribute in a much broader way to the running of the centre, and to make it a broader, more imaginative contribution, most of them either couldn't or wouldn't, and with some it was the latter. They just weren't interested, and boy we tried!

Presumably some of those department heads had spent many years fulfilling their role in a particular way?

Yes, I think so, and nobody had asked them to look at the organization in a broader way, and nobody had suggested that their contribution was not just to do their job but to think much more broadly about what they did. So, as a board of directors, we realized that this wasn't working. We had tried to share the roles and responsibilities with the department heads, but they weren't interested. But that process itself was useful, in the sense that quite a number of the department heads chose to leave over the next year or so anyway. There were only a few that we had to part company with. We then recruited a completely new tranche of about 15 departmental heads, and forged a new relationship with them, which is the very open relationship that we have now.

Presumably you were looking for a very different type of person when you were recruiting the new department heads?

Yes, absolutely. We wanted people who were, of course, technically excellent, who were also good managers and who were people who were ready to contribute to the broader vision of what the Barbican was about.

Planning change

I was intrigued when Sir John mentioned that he hadn't appreciated the extent of the crisis at the Barbican when he took on the role of leading it. I wanted to know how soon it was before he did realize, and how quickly he developed a plan to do something about it. I wanted to know how much planning went into the change programme at the Barbican, and what the strategy was. Who was involved? How was the plan received? What obstacles stood in the way?

I think you began by saying that when you arrived at the Barbican in 1995, you didn't appreciate the extent of the crisis. At what stage did you start to form the vision of what the Barbican could, and should, be like? At what stage was the plan developed?

I remember in the first six months setting out a timetable for how all the facilities needed to be revamped. It set out a programme of everything that needed to be changed and how we planned to do it. And I remember presenting it to my committee, who are the supervisory board, and I could tell, even as I was doing it, that this was just water off a duck's back. They were never going to fund it. They didn't take it seriously. This was just not what the place was about. It was a complete waste of time.

So then slowly we realized that they would never 'buy' a strategic plan. We were helped by the fact that the building was getting older and all sorts of bits needed replacing. It always seemed to be the air-handling units! So at each stage we argued that there was no point spending £2 million on air-handling units in the theatre if you don't then also take the opportunity to do other things as well.

Once that process began, as a matter of fact in the theatre, the next time it was easier to make the same argument about the concert hall, the art gallery, and so on. So when you look through what's happened over the last ten years there was one major project more or less every year. When you look back on it, it looks like a deftly structured ten-year programme of change. True, it was very pragmatic, but it was driven by a very practical sense that this had to be done, firstly, and while we were doing that, we had to improve the facilities. So there has been a kind of super-pragmatism to it.

Then I suppose there was a stage when we had improved all the facilities, when we realized that we had to do all the bits in between. For example, the foyers, the new entrance, and all the other areas that are where the value was going to be added. So by that stage, and that's probably only about four years ago, it was then clear what the remaining elements of the strategy ought to be.

And these final changes are what have created the impression that the Barbican is a single arts complex, rather than a theatre, a concert hall, a gallery and so on?

If that's the impression, then that's terrific! That is what it was intended to do, of course. But although we knew that an enormous amount needed to be done, we also knew that the nature of the funding was such that there was no point in asking for a single, large sum of money. The Corporation would have just freaked! So there was, I suppose, a tactical canniness on our part. We have made the changes to the Barbican in bite-sized chunks, driven by practicality and necessity.

And presumably that's why you chose not to close the Barbican during any development phase, but to keep virtually everything open at all times.

Yes, because that would have been too much of a risk. The organization was too young. If we had suggested that we needed to close for a couple of years, it would have killed the programme of renovation and innovation stone dead. So that was a very deliberate strategic position. We would soldier through, because even with bits of the place filled with scaffolding and hoardings, the art was still going on, and the arts were still evolving.

So that was a very important position – and over ten years, the arts were transformed, the building has been transformed, the way in which the organization was run has been transformed, and I suppose there have been three conveyor belts running at slightly different speeds, but they are always running in exactly the same direction, and in the end all of them now, I think, are about where we wanted them to be.

You described the regeneration of the Barbican as a series of tactics, and in a way the arts and performances have evolved from an opportunity created by the Royal Shakespeare Company moving out. I get the impression that there was a lot of chance involved in the process. What role do you think you have played in this series of tactics and chance?

That impression of chance would be misleading!

Well I rather expected that was the case.

My key relationship has been with Graham Sheffield, the Artistic Director. From the time the RSC left, Graham said that we had to have a new kind of theatre, a new kind of programming. It would be international, so there would be a number of visiting companies, and it would be multi art-form. So the development of the arts was driven by that very strong vision – there was no chance involved in that.

I think that as far as the music programming was concerned, our core was the London Symphony. Then when the BBC Symphony was brought on board, that extended the repertoire by about 50 years, roughly. Then in our own programming, the Great Performance was doing the Baroque and the high quality international, so that also fitted. Then our relationships with promoters such as Cyrius gave us another element. Admittedly, there was an element of the opportune with the BBC Symphony. They came to us because they were being indifferently treated at the Festival Hall. Our music people realized what this would add. It wasn't simply another resident orchestra, it was an associate orchestra which was doing a completely different type of artistic programming, so it gave our music programme coherence just as the theatre programme had coherence.

Then by the time we took over the art gallery, which was only six years ago, we looked at what we were doing in the theatre and music, and asked ourselves what was the equivalent in the art gallery? That needed quite a shift, but now, in the last 18 months, I think we are there, and so the gallery programming is going to have a similar kind of feel.

Do you see the South Bank arts centre as your chief rival, your chief competitor?

Yes, it must be. But it is a very different beast because it is a coalition of independent units.

But surely that's how people regarded the Barbican ten years ago?

That's right, yes. And now we have much more artistic editorial control over what we put on in all the venues. That has changed, and that is best shown in the amount of box office risk. Ten years ago it was about £600,000, and now it's nearer £7 million. So that reflects the amount of artistic control, input and risk that we have now.

The impact of change

Organizational change affects people. It's generally accepted that some people handle and manage change better than others. From a personal perspective, I have worked with some people who relish the chance to change something, to try something new, and with others who live in constant fear and dread of the next change to be cast upon them.

There have been a number of studies into organizational change recently. The last Chartered Management Institute poll, for example, revealed that 89 per cent of managers had experienced some sort of organizational change in the last 12 months, and more than 50 per cent had experienced more than three major changes over the past year.

I wondered how Sir John Tusa viewed the way that organizational change affects its people? What lessons has he learned about reducing the impact of change on people? Sir John had already described the need simply to endure the culture of suspicion at the Barbican whilst changes were being made to the senior management team. But what about the changes whose impact was felt by the remaining Barbican staff?

I asked Sir John if he believed that organizational change was just a part of running a business?

Yes, but as far as structural change is concerned, we have only had two. Only twice have we had a significant reorganization of some divisions. That's still plenty though!

Otherwise, the key areas of the arts division and its structure have been pretty stable. So have our people been subjected to change? Apart from what I have said about the way in which the arts themselves change, I'm not sure that they have.

I suppose people handle change in different ways. Some people just can't deal with change, whilst others take it in their stride and some even thrive on it. You come across as someone remarkably comfortable with the changes that you have made and the processes that you have introduced. Is that fair?

That's because I've made them!

But even implementing change presumably causes stress. Are you someone who suffers from stress?

Oh I thrive on it. Parts of what we've done have been stressful. Mainly, I would rather call them *interesting*. What I do dislike is having things which don't work. The frustration of something which is clearly not working is very much greater than the incidental stress that may appear from implementing a change. The two big reorganizations that we have had, have come from my colleagues. I've been aware that they have been needed, but the real push has come from my colleagues. Rightly or wrongly, that is how it has happened. But it hasn't been me saying, 'Right, we're going to do something different today. We're going to create this, that and the other'. So I think that suggests that there was an organic need for it.

You've got 250 people at the Barbican. When changes are implemented – whether they are programming

changes, structural changes or development of the physical structure of the buildings – a lot of people find any change very, very stressful. How do you motivate 250 people to have faith in you, come with you, keep going, live through the change?

Well the important thing is that most of the change, and the need for the change, is first of all understood and identified at quite close to operational level. Take, for example, the services division. That's everything from the people who tear the tickets, to the bar and catering and so on. The need or the wish to change the quality of service came from within that division. I was only vaguely aware that certain things didn't work. But they are driving the change.

Now that is not to say that there weren't a lot of people who have had to change the way they work. That is true. But it has not been a top-down thing. It has been a need for change that has come from within the particular operational area, and when the change has been announced, and we have all said this is going to be difficult, this is going to be sensitive, this is going to upset people, the reaction of at least half the people, and sometimes more, has been, 'Thank goodness you've done it!' So, far from staff finding that sort of change difficult, it actually liberates them.

So they would say that you listened to them?

Yes. That makes the stress much easier to bear. The stress comes from being run inefficiently, or being run rigidly. You know that you want to be providing a different kind of service at a different level, but the rigidities prevent you from doing it.

That's where the stress is. The liberation is when you get rid of that.

So how did your approach compare with the way you ran the BBC World Service? From a cultural perspective, was there not more of a hierarchical structure at the BBC which would have made the open way that you have managed the Barbican almost impossible?

I think the BBC World Service was 2,500 people: Many more layers, many more departments, and 50 nationalities, which added another dimension. Change is actually easier at the Barbican because it is smaller, and once you have identified what the vision and the mission are, and they are all consistent and coherent with what people believe, then change becomes much easier to deliver, because it is coming from inside. I think that was never quite the situation at the World Service. I have probably forgotten how difficult it was.

An organization the size of the Barbican can be quite light on its feet. I mean the Barbican, and the people there, is a rather clever institution. And that cleverness is distributed and stored very widely.

You mentioned that the two organizational changes that you have implemented achieved what was intended. Would you have known along the way that they were heading in the right direction? Would you have known if it was working, or if something was going wrong?

Oh it was very clear. The fact that I needed a bit of persuading that the change was necessary sometimes meant that it was probably introduced a little bit later than my colleagues would have wanted, but what that certainly meant was that the reasons for making the case had become really apparent and the case been made. So in each case, it was very apparent by the time the change was made that it was going to work.

So what is the biggest change you have made at the Barbican, the one that has had the greatest impact?

How people behave and how we treat people. It's as simple as that.

OK, if I was a Barbican employee ten years ago, and I survived the changes and had grown with the Barbican under Sir John Tusa, what would I notice now? How would I be treated differently now?

There is much more information on an absolutely regular and systematic basis. So you would know that there is a monthly staff letter, you would know that there are three-monthly staff meetings, monthly core briefs, and an annual AGM, which we have just had. That's where I reviewed the last ten years, the last year and then the next five years. So the atmosphere is completely different.

There is much less sense of hierarchy. There is a much greater sense of responsibility. We are constantly pushing responsibility downwards.

Presumably that means much more reliance on the integrity and skill of the team leaders?

Oh yes. And there are some comparatively junior people who take big decisions. For example, our web designer. In hierarchy terms, she is relatively low down, but she is an absolute genius web designer, and if you consider that our face to the world shines through that website, then that is a fantastic degree of responsibility. But nobody worries about that. Nobody questions why such a junior person is carrying that amount of responsibility. She is just so good at her job that you would be a fool not to give her her head.

All those things you would notice as having changed from ten years ago. It's just about how you treat people, how you talk to people. From our point of view, it's all terribly simple. I think it's not being frightened of being open. There are a lot of organizations which are really frightened about openness. I will just give you one example of this. We are planning a book about the twenty-fifth birthday of the Barbican. We need an article by a theatre critic about whether the RSC was right to leave. And people said, 'Do you really want to air that?' And I replied that if we didn't air it, then someone else will. I'm not frightened of the answers. Some of our lords and masters over at the Corporation were almost panic-struck at the thought! My view is that it's there, it happened, it was a crisis – it is a part of the history.

Communication and culture

Many of the techniques, and much of the advice Sir John Tusa had offered for managing people through change seemed to centre on the importance of communication. Yet he had not used the word 'communication' once in our discussion. I wondered whether my attempt to group together these tools under this single banner was being too simplistic.

You describe the procedures that you have introduced as very simple. The staff letters, the staff meetings, the core briefs. They all seem to be about communication?

Yes. It goes hand-in-hand, side-by-side, with the view of how I treat people. It applies formally, and with face-to-face communication as well. We needed the formal methods of communication because some of my colleagues needed to learn that there was nothing frightening about being open as well. So I think that is something that I personally brought in, and that also comes from (a) being a journalist, (b) having come to management very late and (c) having done all these things for the BBC World Service as well.

I was going to ask you about that. You have introduced massive changes in 11 years at the Barbican, but you lived through even greater cultural change at the BBC throughout the 1980s and early 1990s. How do they compare?

I think what I did at the BBC World Service was very similar to the Barbican, except that when I took the World Service over it was not in a state of crisis. It was a great institution which was waiting to have a lot of latent energy released.

Were you aware of that at the time?

Oh yes, and I had been aware of that from the outside as well. Equally, there were a lot of people at the World Service who were perfectly happy to go on doing what they had been doing for the previous 20 to 25 years, and thought that that was all that needed doing. But the challenges were the same, in the sense that you needed to have the right directors, and you have to look at your staff and identify the ones who are just running on auto-pilot and the ones who are capable of managing and editing in a more contemporary and imaginative, human way. And so that process took place at the World Service, just as it has taken place at the Barbican. But I suppose there was a really big challenge to get the organization to start thinking about itself, and what it wanted to be. As it was a much older institution, it had its history, it knew what it did, it knew what it had done, it knew what its past was about. But it wasn't as good at knowing what it *wanted* to be, and what needed to change in order to become that.

Now, it is perfectly obvious that the way I approach change could not be more different from the way in which change came to the BBC under Director-General John Birt, after I left. That was a much more top-down system, which, as you well know, was regarded as not being the way you run that sort of institution. But there are others who were there at the time who say that a lot of necessary change was introduced. All I can do is to express and speak up for the style of change management which goes with the institution's standards, with the human values of people, and which I believe also expresses the sort of person that I am. So I think it is important to *like* people quite a lot! I think that bosses don't always give the impression that they do.

Given that John Birt's successor, Greg Dyke, couldn't have been *less* of a top-down person, do you think that Greg Dyke was better suited for the role?

Oh yes I think much, much more so, because he understood what the BBC's values were. I think that one of the really important things about transformation is that you, as the chief executive, must have an idea of the sort of organization you have come to run, but you then need to understand the sort of organization that it actually is. You may have an outside view, but you also need to discover what the inside view is, and then put those two together. Changes may be required, but if what you are doing is running completely across the internal value systems, then you are in big trouble.

At the Barbican, it took a little time before we thought we were in a position to devise what our vision and mission was. It was there, it was latent, but it wasn't ready. It was only when we felt that it was ready to articulate that we then went through that process. But it was certainly not a question of marching in and announcing what the organization was going to be, what the vision and the mission were, and telling the people to get on and do it.

So had the vision for the Barbican never been articulated before?

No. It was very difficult to articulate a vision when so much of the art that you put on was not under your control. The art gallery was run by someone else. The RSC ran the theatre, and by and large what we did in the concert hall was fairly minor. It was only when we had got control of the arts programming that we could consider, and then articulate, what we genuinely stood for.

Is that control over the arts programming what the South Bank Centre still lacks? Is that the distinction between the South Bank and the Barbican?

Yes, I think that has always been the distinction, and I think that that will continue to be seen as the distinction.

It's interesting to see how our department heads, and others, see the distinction between the South Bank and the Barbican. They regard us as rather lean and sharp, and of course we are actually very broad-based. We are very diverse, we are not elite at all, and we are a bit experimental, radical even. So I think if you asked many of my senior colleagues if they thought the word 'cuddly' applies to us, they would say absolutely not! We aren't cuddly, we do not want to be cuddly, and by and large those are the values which are being expressed at the South Bank.

Looking to the future

Sir John Tusa is in an unusual position, insofar as he has already announced his retirement, and the search for his successor has begun. I wondered whether he could look back at the changes he had introduced and see a pattern? Is he proud of what his tenure achieved at the Barbican? What sort of person does he think should replace him and what advice would he offer them?

So the Barbican's twenty-fifth anniversary is next year – 2007? Are you proud of the Barbican, and what it is now?

Hugely!

I understand that the recruitment of your successor has already started. What sort of person do you think would be effective?

Well I think it needs to be quite a searching process, and probably quite an uncomfortable one. It's tempting to assume that there is nowhere obvious to go now, because people say we run the best arts programme in the world. My view is that just because you are the best, it doesn't mean that you can't get better.

So let's imagine that it's the middle of July next year and your successor has been identified. It's only charitable to take him or her out to lunch. What advice would you offer them?

You have to have the big vision for five years, and you have to stand up and say it, and you say it to everybody. Otherwise they will assume that everything is just chugging along in exactly the same way. After all, it works so well, why do we have to change? You really have to question what you need to change and why, rather than just sit on your laurels.

So your advice to anyone who needs to implement change would be to communicate?

Oh yes, communication is absolutely essential. You cannot go back on things like that. Communicate, and also delegate. You see, the interesting thing is that some of the departmental heads here are now almost fulfilling directorate roles, and they are certainly showing director-type behaviour.

It sounds as if, whilst the approach to implementing change is relatively straightforward, the institution itself has remained as complex now as it ever was?

Well nowadays there are so many more opportunities for what you can do. For example, our relations with all of our neighbouring arts institutions are now much richer. We are probably going to integrate the administration with the Guildhall School of Music and Drama; we may even end up in a full merger in two or three years' time. Then there's the whole question of how we relate to the 2012 London Olympics, and that's another big, big subject.

In other words, the opportunities in all the things we are working on mean that a really ambitious strategic growth is now possible. It wasn't possible ten years ago because we were struggling to survive.

I read a quotation of yours, that 'Management is all about asking questions rather than answering them'. We've looked at many of the skills required to manage change in an organization, but presumably

you would add that you need to have the ability to question the need for change in the first place?

I think that's right. Funnily enough, at the end of my recent presentation to staff at our AGM, I said something quite similar – I said that it's not shameful to miss targets, but it is an error not to set them. And that's what my successor must do. As I said earlier, we couldn't do that ten years ago, because our only mission was to survive. But because of where we are now, we need some very bold targets and vision.

You must be very anxious about who will be recruited to succeed you?

The other day my assistant asked me if I minded who my successor was. I only thought of the right answer yesterday. I should have said, 'I don't mind, but I do care!' I don't mind in a possessive way, but I will care if they balls it up!

Conclusions and recommendations

Before meeting Sir John Tusa, I had read an article in *The Times* which had described his 'effortlessly powerful presence'. 'The word "gravitas"', the article continued, 'could have been invented for Sir John Tusa'. The journalist who wrote the article had been absolutely right. It's not difficult to see why people are prepared to listen to what he has to say, and to follow him willingly along the path that he chose for the Barbican Arts Centre. His combination of calmness, dignity and charm – which makes him such a fascinating person to talk to – is matched by his eagerness to actually get up and get going with the job in hand. That, I believe, is why every organization would want to turn to Sir John Tusa in a crisis. Plenty of leaders can offer you sane and pragmatic advice. Sir John is one, but he would also harness everyone's support and commitment, make them feel completely in control of the situation, and then get on with dealing with it.

Sir John's legacy is a formidable one. He has transformed the Barbican in his 11 years as Managing Director. Together with his Artistic Director, Graham Sheffield, he has recreated and relaunched the entire performing and visual arts programme. All this, while every venue at the Barbican, from the concert hall to the theatre and art gallery, has been redeveloped and improved.

So how has it happened? Sir John's own view is remarkably straightforward: 'I have simply set a course, knowing that my colleagues will deliver.' It clearly has not been as easy to deliver as it has to describe. In an interview with *The Telegraph*, he described the Barbican he entered as 'a shambles. Nobody trusted anyone. It took four to five years of slowly grinding things through before we began to feel it was anything other than immensely hard work. I was on a three-year contract and I can tell you I thought very hard about renewing it'. Once the scale of the challenge had sunk in, the reality of what has happened involved earning the trust of his people, sharing the vision with them of what the Barbican could be, and then involving them in the process every step of the way.

As with so many effective leaders, part of Sir John's leadership success can be attributed to his energy and passion for the arts. He is known to work very long hours, but admits that he doesn't regard what he does as work, rather as 'sheer pleasure'. His passion is such that when his tenure at the Barbican was extended by 18 months, it seemed almost like a reward for his ten years of hard work. After all, it will ensure that he will see through the final phase of redevelopment, and then be around to join in the Barbican's twenty-fifth birthday celebrations in March 2007. In his own words 'this will mark the completion of everything I have wanted to achieve for the institution'.

Managing change checklist

If you are considering change for your organization, or are leading a team of people through change, here are some issues to think about. You might want to find a few, valuable minutes to take a clean sheet of paper and jot down any ideas that the following list generates.

Be aware of change around you
Is your organization adapting to the changing needs of your customers or marketplace? In what ways are your customers changing their behaviour? What mechanisms do you have in place for keeping track of what your customers or stakeholders want?

How do you view change?
If a crisis occurred in your organization, would you view it as an opportunity or a catastrophe? What would be the equivalent of the RSC moving out for you? What would you do if your biggest customer went elsewhere? What steps can you take to ensure that you treat a challenge to your business as an opportunity for change?

Managing conflict
Are you kidding yourself that things are bound to get better? What are you putting up with? Is it time for you to take some brave but necessary decisions in order to move forward?

Being open

Where do the ideas for change originate in your organization? Is change being driven by your staff, your customers, or your senior management team? To what extent do you involve your staff in the strategic change process? What are your staff telling you needs to be changed? Are you open and honest with your staff about the need for change, and its likely impact on the people concerned?

People and change

Do you view a member of staff leaving your organization as a problem, or as an opportunity to review your requirements? What can you do to minimize the stress and unease that strategic changes cause? Have you always kept lines of communication open with your people? What roles and responsibilities can you push down to your more junior staff?

Planning change

Are the changes you plan to implement a series of tactics? Are they part of a wider strategic plan? How would you know if a specific change you have made is having the effect that you planned? Can you measure the effects of the change? Who are the key colleagues around you whom you can rely on for support?

Culture

Do you think that you need to consider changing the culture of your organization? If a client or customer walked into your office or building, what impression would they get of you and your organization? Would they think that it looks like a great place to work? What changes do you need to make? Where do you plan to start?

Your biggest change

What is the biggest change that you have ever had to make? What could you have done better with hindsight? What lessons have you learned?

Lord Karan Bilimoria on meeting customer needs

Lord Karan Bilimoria, Founder and Chief Executive of Cobra Beer

'Most business ideas come from being dissatisfied with a product or service and thinking, "I can do this better and I can do this differently, and ideally I can change the marketplace I am going into forever".'

Lord Karan Bilimoria's career is a remarkable one. Having graduated in law from Cambridge University in 1988 and qualified as a chartered accountant with what is today Ernst & Young, he turned his attention to developing a less gassy, premium lager brewed to appeal to both ale drinkers and lager drinkers alike, and to complement spicy food. Little more than 15 years later, Cobra Beer is one of the fastest growing beer brands in the UK and one of the most innovative young companies in the country. The brand has a current retail value turnover of £96 million, is sold in nearly 6,000 Indian restaurants, and is available to 6,000 bars, pubs and clubs and in leading multiples, supermarkets and off-licenses throughout the UK.

Cobra Beer was awarded 12 Gold Medals at the 2006 Monde Selection, Brussels, World Selection of Quality Awards – more than any other beer in the world and one more than the company's already world-beating total in 2005.

Although Karan started Cobra in 1990 when he was, by his own admission, 'up against all odds', Cobra has grown into an operation with offices on four continents and exports to over 45 countries, with brewing operations in five countries. Needless to say, he is widely respected for his entrepreneurial spirit. Karan is the Representative Deputy Lieutenant of the London Borough of Hounslow and among many other positions serves as Chancellor of Thames Valley University – the UK's youngest at the time of his appointment. Karan is one of the first two Visiting Entrepreneurs ever appointed at Cambridge University, serves as National Champion of the National Council for Graduate Entrepreneurship, and is a Champion of the Enterprise Insight Make Your Mark campaign. He sits on the Government's National Employment Panel (NEP), and from 2001 to 2005 was Chairman of the

NEP's SME Board. Additionally, Karan serves as UK Chairman of the Indo British Partnership and Vice-Chairman of the London Chamber of Commerce and Industry's Asian Business Association, and sits on the UK-India Round Table and the Asia Task Force. He lectures extensively in the UK and abroad on entrepreneurship, business, education and the Indo–British relationship.

Karan also directly supports a number of charities, serving as a patron of the Thare Mache Starfish Initiative, a patron of Rethink severe mental illness, and as Chairman of the advisory board of the Shrimati Pushpa Wati Loomba Memorial Trust for the education of children of poor widows in India. He is Chairman of the Memorial Gates Committee and a member of the Advisory Council of CIDA Foundation UK.

Karan has won numerous awards in recognition of his business achievements and charitable work, including the RSA's Albert Medal in the Society's 250th anniversary year, 2004, and a CBE in the Queen's Honours List for 2004. He was named Entrepreneur of the Year 2003 and Business Person of the Year 2004 by the London Business Awards, Entrepreneur of the Year 2004 at the National Business Awards (London and South East of England) and London Entrepreneur of the Year 2003 (Consumer Products) by Ernst & Young. In 2005, Karan was honoured with the Award for Outstanding Achievement by the Institute of Chartered Accountants in England and Wales in the Institute's 125th anniversary year. He was named Man of the Year at the 2006 Drinks Business Awards. He has been awarded honorary doctorates by Brunel University, Heriot-Watt University and Staffordshire University.

In June 2006, Karan was appointed The Lord Bilimoria, of Chelsea.

I had been looking forward to meeting Karan Bilimoria, because everything I had heard about the way he established and developed Cobra Beer presented a conundrum. Here was a young qualified chartered accountant, working for one of the world's most prestigious accountancy practices. A law graduate from Cambridge University. Severely hampered, however, by debts of more than £20,000, which he had accumulated as a student and while he was qualifying as an accountant. Yet he decides to leave the City to establish what he was always confident would be a global beer brand. All this without any brewing or retail-sector experience at all. By his own admission, he'd never even pulled a pint.

Now, I've met a few accountants in my time, and they're not known for their willingness to take risks. I was reminded of the Monty Python sketch where an accountant takes careers advice because he had decided that what he really wants is to be a circus lion tamer. It seemed to me that, on paper at least, Karan Bilimoria's career path was only marginally more sensible.

So what sort of person is prepared to take such a leap of faith? Most of us have an idea at one stage or another, which we believe could be turned into a profitable business or venture. And yet so few of us do anything about it. Why is Karan Bilimoria so different? What qualities or skills enabled him to follow what, to most of us, would be an idle dream? I needed to find out.

I was particularly pleased to be interviewing Karan on the subject of meeting customer needs. Nowadays, ever more emphasis is placed on the importance and nature of the relationships that an organization has with its customers. Indeed, an array of software applications and university course modules have been developed in recent years in the discipline of Customer Relationship Management (CRM). So for a consumer brand like

Cobra, I wanted to know how Karan Bilimoria had set out to meet his customers' needs. How close was he to his customers at the start, and how close does he think Cobra is now?

Market and customer research

I wanted to start by going back to the very early days of Cobra. Let's put aside for the moment the student debt, and the seemingly impossible personal circumstances that Cobra's founder found himself in. I knew that he had no brewing experience at the time, but how well did he know his future customers? How did he know that his experience of drinking gassy lager with spicy food was the same as everyone else's? What customer research, formal or otherwise, had he conducted before concluding that Cobra was the answer?

I have read a number of interviews that you have given, as well as several articles about you, and what comes across is that there seems to have been a lot of luck involved at the start. I'd really like to know what research you did back in 1989 to see whether your experience of gassy lagers with spicy food was the same as everyone else's. What testing did you do to see if they suited anybody else's palate?

Most business ideas come from being dissatisfied with a product or service and thinking, 'I can do this better and I can do this differently, and ideally I can change the marketplace I am going into forever'. Another way of putting it is that you feel passionately about something on the one hand, and really hate something on the other. In my case, I've just always loved beer from the time I was allowed to drink it. However, when I came to this country from India as a 19-year-old, for my higher education, I took an instant dislike to the famous lager brands that I was trying out over here. As a customer, I just found them very difficult to drink – very gassy, very fizzy. Then an English friend of mine introduced me to real ale, which I loved – to this day I still love it. But the problem I found was that although I love all food, in particular I used to miss my Indian food. I couldn't cook when I came here, and I would go to Indian restaurants and eat spicy food, and I would want something cold and refreshing to drink. That's why lager is the most popular drink in Indian restaurants, because it is meant to be cold and chilled and refreshing. But it was also gassy, fizzy, bloating, harsh, bland – a very uncomfortable combination with the Indian food. And I thought that all these ale and lager drinkers must be going through the same experience that I am. They want to drink ale, but ale doesn't go well with Indian food. It's too heavy, too bitter. Or they want to drink something cool and refreshing, but instead they get these bland, fizzy, bloating lagers. I also realized that, as a customer, the restaurant owner could be selling me more beer and more food.

A good business idea is often customer-driven, from the experience of being a customer yourself. Then this idea evolved during my visits to my family in India in my holidays when I was studying at Cambridge. I was doing my law degree then. Even when I was working to qualify as an accountant with Ernst & Young in the City, every year I would work overtime. I wouldn't take it as money, I would take it as extra holiday so that I could go and see my family in India and visit my father – who was a general in the army – wherever he was posted. It was on these visits to India that I actually came up with the idea. It was not a

'Eureka' moment, but the idea evolved that one day I would bring over my own beer over from India. It would be a lager and have all the refreshing qualities of a lager but it would be less gassy, it would be smoother, it would accompany Indian food and it would appeal to ale drinkers. So that was my idea. Of course, making the idea a reality is what it is all about. Enterprise means coming up with ideas and putting them into action – that is what entrepreneurship really is all about. So of course the thing is actually to go out and do it.

But to answer your question, the idea evolved from being a customer myself. So when you talk about being consumer-driven, well, we are all consumers.

Absolutely. But your background was in accounting, you were working at Ernst & Young at the time?

Well I actually did a degree in India. Then I did a diploma here for a year, then I did my articles and qualified as a chartered accountant, and then I went to Cambridge and did my law degree in two years instead of three. I got a year's exemption, so I had to squeeze it into two years. After I graduated from Cambridge I worked for six months in the City and then I realized, this just isn't for me. Being a qualified chartered accountant and a law graduate, the career route that I should have taken was mergers and acquisitions, corporate finance, investment banking – and for six months I had been toying with that. Then I realized no, I want to start my own business, I want to do my own thing. I want that freedom of opportunity. I want that limitless opportunity. I want to be in control of my own destiny. I want the freedom to do what I want to, when I want to, and I had this one big idea, and so I decided to take the plunge.

I teamed up with a partner who was a childhood friend of mine who also wanted to start his own business.

For six months I helped out a friend as director of his company, called European Accounting Focus. I wasn't a salesman, I had never had any sales or marketing training, but I ended up being Sales and Marketing Director because I spotted an opportunity and I sold the magazine subscriptions, did all the marketing for him, and took it from almost zero to selling several hundred subscriptions a month. So I discovered that I had the ability to sell. When I was at Cambridge, I became Vice-President of the Union, and for the elections I would go door-to-door canvassing. You weren't allowed to send out leaflets, so you had to go door-to-door. You were selling yourself, and getting complete strangers you had never met before to vote for you. I realized pretty quickly that with selling, there is one thing that there is no shortcut to, and that is hard work. Up and down the staircases, whether it was raining or snowing, on your bike – just going and doing it. So I learned about sales. I learned I had the ability to sell, which in my book is the key asset that you need in business.

So if you are setting up in business you need to be able to sell?

I think it is one of the most important skills in life. That's something that was apparent when I was one of the judges on a programme called 'The Big Idea', on Sky TV, where budding entrepreneurs are given the chance to show their inventions to a panel of business experts for a chance to secure investment in their idea. When all the ideas were presented to us, invariably these inventors' ideas were from their own personal experiences of not being happy with something, or realizing that something could be done differently, or wondering why somebody isn't doing this a different way. And often they are very simple ideas.

I think you're right. And yet, when I watch inventors pitch their ideas on 'Dragons' Den', the BBC television programme where entrepreneurs pitch their ideas to well-known businesspeople, the panel seem to be looking for sales forecasts and research about the size of their market. The passion and the belief of the individual seem almost incidental. Were you not concerned about those things at the start? Presumably your background in accountancy must have prompted you to question them?

Very much so. That's why I knew that my beer idea was a big idea. I knew that it would require a lot of organizing, require financing, and that it had huge potential, because beer is a volume game. To succeed in beer you need to sell lots of it. It is not something you do in a small way if you want to create a serious business. So I knew that from the beginning. And that's why I didn't embark upon it straightaway. That's why I started by importing polo sticks, fashion garments, leather and silk products, furnishings and fabrics from India – we went down lots of dead-ends trying to build up the agency to be the biggest towel company in India, but we realized that we were not able to compete with the Portuguese. We were not able to compete on quality, although in India they were the best and biggest, and we thought that would be enough. But in reality we couldn't make it happen. I could give you several examples of dead-ends that we went down. But all the time you are building experience.

And the idea for the beer was in the back of your mind all this time?

It was there, waiting. And the lucky part of it came with a surprise introduction to the brewery, when I was actually looking to import seafood! But if you don't have the idea to start off with, then the luck doesn't come. Luck is only there if you can feed on it.

Would you say that it was 'opportunity' rather than 'luck'?

It is like serendipity. Mark de Rond, the professor at Cambridge who wrote a case study on Cobra, defined serendipity as seeing what everyone else sees, but thinking what no one else has thought. To me, that is what insight is. People talk about foresight, people talk about vision. My great-grandfather, who started his own business from scratch in India, has always been a great inspiration to me, and I remember that people always said that the secret of his success was foresight. And that term foresight didn't really mean anything to me at the time, but I've come to realise from my own experience that business really is all about vision. I realized that actually it is this ability to spot niches, to spot gaps. In fact, it's more than that. It is spotting a gap in the market and a market in the gap. You know, niches can be very big. So a niche could lead to your business becoming a mainstream brand and that is exactly what Cobra's strategy always was. We intended to start off with Indian restaurants and to use that as a foundation and a base from which to springboard into the mainstream. I had a list. I actually made out a list of my ten business ideas, and right up there at the top was the beer idea. The big one.

Testing

I knew exactly what I wanted the beer to taste like. And it was all from my own experiences, because in those days when I felt like having a lager in a pub, there were small quantities of bottled German beers that had come over and I found them so much more drinkable than the gassy, fizzy pints that were served. So that is what I used to drink, and I can remember these barmen who used to look at me as if I was this mad guy, when I would ask for two bottles of Pils and a pint glass and I would pour them in. I was experimenting all the time, and of course in India the lagers tend to be textured, because there is rice over there as well, in the way they are brewed. So I remembered my Indian lager taste as well, and that love of real ale. So I wanted the quality of an ale and the feel of an ale, and the idea kept developing.

So you knew, when you tasted it, whether it would be right or not? You had this flavour in your mind?

Yes. When I worked with a brew master in India – and again, this was luck – I happened to team up with the largest independent brewery in India. It was family-owned, so I wasn't going to be dealing with one manager who would be posted out or change jobs. They were successful, very successful. They had never exported beer. Their biggest selling brand was a strong lager. They didn't brew a premium lager. They didn't have the sort of beer I wanted. They didn't have a brand name that I could have used, otherwise I would have been an agent or a distributor.

So my partner and I literally created the brand from scratch, the beer from scratch, everything from scratch. I did a lot of research and there is no shortcut for that. Although I knew nothing about brewing beer and had never sold a bottle of beer in my life, we started in September 1989, I went to India in February 1990, and the first container arrived in June 1990. So it took almost a year from the time we started working on the project in earnest to the product actually coming out.

Then we went through another six months of feedback and development on the taste and the quality, based on consumer feedback here. At first it was a little bit too heavy, a little too sweet, so we would get that feedback and slowly adapt, but that basic formula was there, and so we just kept slowly tweaking it and that took about six brews. By December 1990 we had stabilized the taste and we have never changed it since then. So, well over a year of pre-production, production, post-production – and all the time you are starting with the customer. The research we did over here was intensive – huge amounts of research.

I understand the research you undertook with the flavours and the tasting sessions during the development phase. But what about before then? Before September 1989, how many people had you shared the idea with? Did you ask friends whether they found lager too gassy to accompany Indian food? Were those the sort of conversations you had? Or were you keeping the idea to yourself at that time? How did you know that your experience was the same as other people's?

Well I knew my ale-loving friends would hate lager. And I saw people struggling in Indian restaurants. I asked myself, 'Why are people drinking these beers?' But it was very much as if you were on your own. A lot of the time – and I am not alone in this, it's true of other entrepreneurs as well – you feel very much that you are on your own and you are seeing something that no one else is seeing. You are the odd one out. An analogy I could use is from 2003, when I was appointed the UK Chairman of the Indo British Partnership by the UK government. Patricia Hewitt appointed me when she was Secretary of State at the DTI. When I was there trying to push for waking British companies up to the opportunities in India, people were just not interested. When I say people – generally within government – with one or two exceptions, there was no interest. No one could see. It was all China. No one wanted to know. I kept saying, 'You have got to put more resources behind this. India has taken off. British business is going to lose out'. Now, finally – and I felt like a lone voice in the wilderness – everyone has woken up. Now all the doors are opening. Now everyone wants to put more resources into it, we had the first India–UK Investment Summit in October 2006 with both Prime Ministers, Dr Manmohan Singh and Tony Blair, taking part in it, the full weight of government behind it – but three or four years ago there was no one.

So again, the thing is to get people to buy into your idea. With government, for example, I knew that although I felt on my own, if I started fighting them, I wouldn't get anywhere. I had to win people over. I had to lobby away at every opportunity and convince people through reason, through argument, through logic, and then literally take people out to India. The head of UK Trade and Investment had never been to India – he had been to China several times. Of course when I got him to go out to India, I was there with him, a big conference with the British High Commission team, and I waited until the end of the first day and I said, 'Now, tell me what you think of India'. He was almost speechless. He said, 'I can't believe this, this is where China was

13 years ago. This is phenomenal. This is a huge opportunity'. Just that one move, taking that one person there, opened the door. Then one door after another started opening.

Branding and consumer testing

There's no question that, to a beer-lover, Cobra is a household name. It's also one of those brands that is instantly recognisable. I had been fascinated to learn, however, that the beer had very nearly been called Panther. What had brought about the change? What role had customers, or potential customers, played in this change of heart.

These days organizations spend hundreds of thousands, if not millions, of pounds on brand names, logos and identities. They use focus groups, panel interviews, high-street polling, and a host of other research methods, to gauge the likely reaction to a name or brand change.

For Karan Bilimoria, circumstances were very different. I wanted to find out where the name Panther had come from, and what had prompted the name change to Cobra.

I've heard you describe the Cobra brand as your greatest asset. I've also read that you almost called it Panther. What happened there?

If I can just give you a bit more background on what went into the decision to start Cobra – when I went to the brewery for my first trip, after all the research was done, I had all the odds stacked against me. I had £20,000 of student debt, the recession had started (although I didn't know it at the time) in

June 1990. We were up against Kingfisher, the biggest Indian beer brand, which had already started to break here, and which had already been brewing for five years. And about nine or ten other Indian beers were trying and failing. The imported beer market in Britain had just started to take off, and of course you are up against giants – the brewery behind Stella Artois was founded in the fourteenth century, while Cobra Beer was founded just over 14 years ago – giants with a history, and it was also the most competitive beer market in the world, because Britain is a free market. So a free market is great – anyone can have a go. The flip-side of that is huge competition. So every major beer around the world is available in Britain, demonstrated by the fact that not one beer in Britain has even 10 per cent market share. Not one brand. So that makes it so, so competitive.

But I did have two factors in my favour. One was the growth of lager. In 1960, just before I was born, the market was 1 per cent lager, 99 per cent ale. By the time we started Cobra in 1990 it was 50 per cent lager, 50 per cent ale. Today it is 75 per cent lager, 25 per cent ale. The reason for that is we have become globalized, because everywhere else in the world, beer is lager. It is as simple as that.

So I had that in my favour. The second thing was that, within that growing lager sector, the fastest growing sector has been premium lagers. So you have also got to see that the consumer is going to want better and better things. Once the consumer tries the premium lager they are not going to drink a standard lager if they can help it, because premium lager invariably tastes so much better, and the quality is better. People, once discovering something better, rarely go back. And with beer being so affordable as a product, even people who are not very wealthy can afford to treat themselves to more expensive lagers. For 30p or 40p more, you are going to get something way, way better. So it is affordable, whereas to go to the other extreme, if you are driving a Ford Escort and you feel like a Bentley, well sorry, you can't do it. And the analogy with a beer – a standard lager and a really super-duper premium beer like Cobra – is the difference between a Ford Escort and a Bentley. So there is that aspect to it. And you expect that the premium lager sector is going to keep growing because you have faith that the customer is always going to want better and better quality and that's what is happening. Generally the bar is raised the whole time. So what's changed in the world in many ways is that from governments being in charge and from manufacturers being the king, with it all being control-driven, command-driven, driven by the government or driven by manufacturers, now it has all turned around. Now the customer is in the driving seat, the customer is king. The customer wants better quality, more variety, more choice and that bar is being raised the whole time.

And how did the Panther story come about?

When I went to India I took with me about 20 different bottles of beer from around the world, very carefully selected. I took them as hand luggage! It was very much as though within each bottle of beer there were characteristics that I liked, and didn't like. Then I did tastings with the brew master in the laboratory, and I would literally go through each bottle and say, right, this beer, I like this aspect of the taste, and in that way I was able to communicate to him the sort of taste that was in my head – I knew exactly what I wanted the actual taste of my product to be. It was an incredible way of doing it, because a lot of those were very famous lager brands which he could relate to, and he had spent six years in the Czech Republic.

So I had the right brewer, the right people, family, personal attention – it was fantastic. But we hadn't chosen the name of the beer. This was one of my first major customer lessons in business: when we chose the name, we decided on Panther. We could have chosen anything. We went through hundreds of names. We had it designed by a British design agency, and we took it back to India. I remember one of my first meetings with the printer of the brewery's labels. I handed him the artwork, and talked to him about the eye of the black panther, a very cool, modern design. I was so occupied getting the liquid right, and developing the product, and the bottles, and with all the other meetings with suppliers and brewers and all the manufacturing, and I quite frankly forgot about the labels.

Of course I needed some form of marketing, but I couldn't afford any, so my only form of marketing was a table card of flimsy white cardboard. My brother had started an advertising agency in Hyderabad. The brewery was in Bangalore – Hyderabad, which is where I was born, is about a one-hour flight away. So, my table card was A5, flimsy cardboard, white colour with green and black printing, because I couldn't afford full colour – and that was my only item of marketing! It told the customer, explaining in an interesting way with a few illustrative drawings, about the beer, where it was from, its heritage, why it was special, the smooth taste. It was information for the customer to be put on restaurant tables. That was my only item of marketing.

So by now you had planned labels and table cards ready to launch Panther. What happened?

Luckily they hadn't been printed! We were two weeks away from bottling. The beer had been developed, brewed and fermented. Then I got a frantic phone call one evening from my partner, who told me that we had a real problem.

We had pre-sold the first container to a distributor in the north of England, in Newcastle, and a distributor in the south. The distributor in the south had, in turn, tried to pre-sell their allotment, and they were finding great difficulty because people didn't like the name Panther. They just didn't warm to the name.

So we had two choices. Either we stuck with the name, and carried on – after all, they had agreed to take it. Or we could change the name. So I said to my partner, 'Just remind me of the second name on the list' ... he pulled up the list and said, 'It's Cobra'. 'Cobra – OK, I remember that', I said. 'You try Cobra, and I'll find out if the labels have been printed. Get back to me ideally tomorrow, but within 48 hours.' So the next morning, I remember going to the printers and luckily they had left things to the last minute.

I was obviously worried about the name change, but by that evening I got a phone call from England telling me that people loved the name Cobra! So we made the decision. We scrapped Panther. I flew to Hyderabad and with my brother's help, with the advertising agency, we designed Cobra from scratch. It delayed the whole project. We actually had to delay the bottling for a while. I lost time, I lost money, but I learned one of my first lessons in business: you come up with the ideas but you never, ever go forward without checking it with the consumer.

And you still maintain that today?

Yes. And of course, as you said, the name Cobra is our most

valuable asset. As a brand name it turned out wonderfully. It is short. It is sharp. It is punchy. It is memorable. It's a global brand name because my mission was always to brew the finest ever Indian beer and to make it a global beer brand, and the taste has to be extra-smooth, be less gassy, so we know it has got great global appeal. Again, we were able to be close to our customers by being headquartered in London, which is probably the most cosmopolitan city in the world and the most international city in the world. I knew that in London I would have the opportunity to get people from all over the world to try Cobra. I knew straightaway that if Japanese, with their lagers, liked the taste of Cobra, and Americans, with their type of very watery lagers, liked the taste, if Germans liked the taste, then I knew that I had an appealing taste. So what better place in the world to get that right than here in London? And it is the most demanding market, a very competitive market. I knew if I could make it a success in London, I could make it a success anywhere in the world. So that global aspect of the brand name also needed to work, it needed to be a brand name that I could use easily anywhere in the world.

Then of course 'Cobra' had this wonderful way of taking you back to India, to that part of the world, without doing it in a corny or an obvious way like 'Maharajah', for example.

The other thing about it is that it's got this great feel about it, because of the brand and the way we've built it, that people think it has been around for over 100 years. Even in those early days people thought it had always been around, and I would meet retired old British army officers who would say things like, 'I remember my time in India, Cobra, it was delicious ...' – even though it didn't exist then! On the other hand, we had this wonderful aspect of the brand where it had this cool, very contemporary feeling. To have both – a feeling of having been around for ever, and a feeling of being cool and contemporary – wonderful!

Customer strategy: knowing who your customers are

For many organizations, particularly those involved in consumer products, their principal customers are not the end users, but rather the retailers and distributors whom they need to gain access to. This was, and still is, true of Cobra. It does not matter how many people prefer the taste of Cobra to other, more gassy beers, if they can't get hold of it. Since Cobra set out to be the beer of choice to accompany spicy, Indian food, the prime customers were clearly to be the owners of the restaurants themselves. Were they the customers who Karan Bilimoria set out to 'court' from the outset? How well formed was Cobra's early sales and marketing strategy? How close was Cobra to its end users, the drinkers, in the early days? I needed to find out.

In those early days, did you see your prime customers as the restaurants or the punters going into the restaurants?

When we started, we knew that the market for Cobra was there in that there are thousands of Indian restaurants in Britain. We knew that Britain had reached a point where curry is very much our 'national dish', and we knew that Cobra was the perfect beer to accompany it. That said, it was still far from easy in the early days, because the truth is that, of course, both the restaurateurs and the customers were our market, but you have to go through the restaurateurs before you can reach the customers. So reaching out to the restaurant owners was very much our first priority.

Like anything, it's sales – you have to sell it to the restaurants so they can sell it to the customers – and we hit a snag right away because many Indian restaurant owners, quite understandably, don't drink. Two-thirds of restaurant owners are Bangladeshi, with the other one-third being Pakistani, Sri Lankan, Nepalese and Indian. A lot of them, for religious reasons, will not drink. But then I learned one of my fundamental lessons because they said: 'Look, it doesn't matter that we don't drink, it is our customers who matter. Leave a couple of bottles. If our regulars like it we will put in our first order. If our wider customers like it we will reorder.' And they put their customers first. That's one of most valuable lessons I've ever learned in business and I will always be grateful to the Indian restaurateurs for teaching me that, and for giving me the chance, as without the support of the Indian restaurants we wouldn't be where we are today.

There's been a lot of talk in recent years about guerrilla marketing and ambient marketing, but the truth is that you can't beat – and you can't avoid – actually just going out and saying, 'look, I've got this product, it's fantastic, you should buy this'. That becomes a lot harder when your customer actually physically doesn't use what you're trying to sell, but as I said, we'd leave bottles behind, we'd ask them to let their regular customers try it, and if the customers liked it the restaurant could call us to order more. It worked beautifully, not only because there was no pressure, but also because it put the beer right where we needed it: in front of the customer, where they could drink it and enjoy it and tell the restaurant owner. So the answer is two-fold: the restaurants were the primary focus, but ultimately it does come down the customer. And this is where your product really, really has to stand up on quality. Because if the end user, your customer's customer, in a way, doesn't like it, then you won't get those reorders.

And how did that fit in your overall strategy?

My game-plan was a very simple one. The game-plan was, first, to establish the brand in the UK. If I could establish in the UK, in the most competitive beer market in the world, I would then know that I had the confidence and the credibility to take it anywhere else in the world, and in particular back to India. It was always my dream to take Cobra 'home', as it were.

So part of my strategy was always to get it back in India when the time was right, and four years ago I thought that the time was right – my vision was that India was going to open up as an economy, and was going to take off and liberalize, and that process actually began shortly after I started Cobra, in 1991. And of course now for the last year-and-a-half we have been manufacturing in India for India – and in the last six months or so in India, it has grown six times. We saw sales double between November and December 2006. Although it's true that we're starting from a small base, that's still very encouraging for us. We started with one brewing facility in January 2005. This year we will have five brewing facilities in India. It's going to be our biggest market looking ahead.

So that was part of the game-plan. The other part of the game-plan was that in Britain I would start with the Indian restaurants, because I knew that everyone goes to Indian restaurants. Whatever social strata people belong to, A, B or C, whatever age group, and whichever part of Britain, people go to Indian restaurants on a regular basis. So I had a very wide customer base.

In the restaurants, I came out with those big 650ml bottles – the bottles themselves were forced on me by the brewery, but I turned that disadvantage into an advantage. This is the way the beer is sold in India – right now, more than 16 years later, more than 90 per cent of beer sold in India is sold in these bottles. What happens is that everyone recycles those bottles; everyone uses the same size and shape of bottle, and they just go round and round the market. They come back and they get recycled. And because we started brewing in India and exporting to the UK, that was our only option. We could only get the 650ml Indian bottles. And we really had to, as I say, turn that disadvantage into an advantage, because initially the restaurants didn't want them. They said, give us 330ml bottles or give us kegs, draught beer. I couldn't make draught in India, and I couldn't get my hands on 330ml bottles. But I knew that we could make those 650ml bottles work because they'd really stand out. Customers would see those 650ml bottles on the tables and ask what they were. They would want to try it. And it would spread like wildfire throughout the restaurant. And also people would share it. It took the weight off the waiters because they would leave the bottles on the table for people to share, and people would enjoy the sharing experience. No one had had the guts to do it before. All the other Indian beers were exported from India in small bottles because they were all told no, the customer in Britain wants small bottles. The customer – meaning the restaurants in this case, the trade – wanted small bottles, and you're actually giving the customer, the end-user, something that they don't want. It turned out that customers loved the bigger bottles, and now everyone uses them.

And I could tell you story after story … For example, there was a launch of a very famous restaurant in London called the Star of India, in Kensington, Earls Court, and they were refurbishing – renaissance murals all over the walls, huge profile, celebrity re-launch with the press there, and they weren't stocking Cobra before the refurbishment of the restaurant. Through a contact, I managed to get the beer sponsorship for the launch. Now it was the evening of the launch, and we sent the beer ahead and I remember I got this frantic phone call from, I think it was my business partner, and I remember him saying, 'He is refusing to take them. "Why these big bottles?" He said "no, I can't take big bottles", he made all the excuses … "I can't take big bottles, we want small bottles", and he is panicking …' And typically, with a big celebrity launch coming up, there were still wires hanging out of the ceiling and he was trying to get the place ready, and he just refused to take delivery. So I got him on the phone and I said – 'Please, you've got too many things to worry about now, don't worry about the beer. I can assure you your customers will love it this evening. It's working, it's selling like hot cakes everywhere, I am getting 100 per cent re-orders from the restaurants, trust me. You concentrate on your opening – just take the delivery, chill it and serve it. I'll be there myself this evening.' I walked into the launch and he had a big smile on his face. Within one hour they ran out of Cobra! He became one of my most loyal customers after that and to this day they serve the big bottles.

So the picture I have is that you knew that ultimately Cobra was a beer for India. You knew

that the UK was where to start, and you knew that the route to the sort of people you needed to get to was via the Indian restaurants in the UK.

Well ultimately I wanted it to be a truly global brand – that was the mission from the start – but yes, I was very keen on taking it back to India, and I knew that because people discovered the product in the Indian restaurants, because of the sharing concept, when they were eventually able to get it on the supermarket shelf, they would recognize it as the beer from the Indian restaurant that they liked so much. Initially they would buy from the supermarket shelf, possibly when they were getting a chilled or frozen takeaway, or when they were cooking an Indian meal at home, or to have with their Indian takeaway that they ordered from their restaurant, and then later they would buy it because they just like the beer. And the next step would be to get into the pubs, the bars, the hotels and the clubs.

So we established a base in the Indian restaurants, then the supermarkets, and in 2006, for the first time, more than 50 per cent of our sales were actually from outside the Indian restaurants. And the Indian restaurants are still growing significantly.

You say that these phased sales were all planned. But back in 1989, did you really know that each of these phases was what you had to go through, or have these stages evolved?

Oh no, I knew. I knew I would have to go through these stages – very much so. There wasn't any other way to do it – the market is just too competitive. We were clever, I think, in spotting a niche and then expanding from it, although sometimes there were temptations just to launch in India straight away. You need the discipline to have patience and take things step by step. If I had released in India as well we would have shot ourselves in the foot because we would have had even more trouble getting hold of the product for the UK.

At any of the stages, have you ever been fundamentally wrong about how you expected your customers to react?

I don't think so – not if you realise how important it is to communicate to your customers what your product is all about. When we defined who the customer is, we recognized that in our case, *everyone* is the customer. Even our suppliers are customers, because everyone drinks Cobra. Everyone you are dealing with is a customer. Everyone who walks into this office is a customer in that sense. Your customer is basically the wider consuming public. I learned this lesson very early, just by observing. I would see businesspeople who would worship their customers, but bully their suppliers and bully their employees. I think that's wrong. We have always treated suppliers and customers equally.

The marketing is crucial as well. It's all about feature and benefit. You have an extra-smooth beer, that's the feature – but so what? It has got to have a benefit. That benefit has got to be a benefit to all the customers down the line. So because it is less gassy and extra smooth and easier to drink, eventually your restaurant owner will sell more food and more beer, so there is a benefit to the restaurant owner. And of course for the consumer, they are having a much better, more pleasant, happier, more comfortable experience and enjoying a better-quality product. So that benefit has got to go all the way down the line – there is no point if only the consumer likes it but the person selling it has a problem in that they don't benefit from it.

The credibility gap: having confidence, passion and belief in your product

I understood the need for Cobra to get across the benefits of their beer at the earliest opportunity. I appreciated the persuasiveness of the argument that Cobra is less gassy, and so will allow diners to both drink and eat more. However, just selling the benefits to its customers wasn't going to turn Cobra into a global brand. So what enabled Cobra to compete effectively with the established drinks brands with six- and seven- and eight-figure marketing budgets? After all, Stella Artois has roots going back almost six and a half centuries. How did Karan Bilimoria set out to sell Cobra's features and benefits to such an established sector? What made it possible for Cobra's David to compete against the established Goliaths?

I call it the 'credibility gap'. This is the term I give especially to organizations in their early days when they are starting out. Nobody knows you, nobody knows your product, nobody knows your brand. What gives people confidence in you? What makes people want to buy from you, to supply you and to finance you when you are in that position? I believe they do those things if you have complete and utter faith, confidence and belief in your product, in your idea and in yourself, because that confidence that you have gives people the confidence to trust you, to give you a chance. So you have got to have that passion and that belief in what you are doing. That comes across to people, and that's what it is in those early days – walking in and getting a bank manager to give you an overdraft when you've got no security, going into a brewery and persuading them to deal with two young guys.

In that first meeting with the brewery, there was a semi-circle of the whole brewery management team, and I was on my own sitting in there, in this intimidatingly huge office. The company secretary, general manager, head brewer, managing director, vice-president, chief accountant, they were all there, and they all individually and collectively laughed in my face. They told me that I didn't stand a chance. They said that I didn't know anything about their industry – I knew nothing about brewing beer, I'd never sold any beer, I had no money, I had no experience. And that's when I was able, in that situation, on my own, to say: 'I am going to succeed. I have faith, I have confidence, I have passion, I have belief in myself, and in my idea. So this is why it's going to work.'

So in your role as a judge on 'The Big Idea' television programme, I get the impression that you were looking for more than an idea. You were also looking for the passion and the confidence of the person behind that idea.

Yes. And you do see it. The two ideas I selected that made it through to the finals both involved inventors with complete and utter dedication. They completely believe in what they are doing.

But when you are judging a new business idea, surely you also need to look at your knowledge of the market, your sales forecasts, your profit margins...?

If I had done a course of analysis before I had started I would have failed on every one of them. My parents called me an import-export wallah. They said, 'All this education, and here you are becoming an import-export wallah! Get a proper job!'

If I had gone to any of the top management consulting firms, they would have told me not to waste my time and theirs. And at the time they would have been absolutely right. We did our first share issue in 1995 under the Enterprise Investment Scheme, before which we had one business agent who had come in and taken 5 per cent of the company in 1993. Then my partner left in 1995, and I bought him out and I sold some shares, and I diluted down to 72 per cent, which is what I held until just recently – I am now at 67 per cent. And I remember that when we had that first share issue there were so many people who turned us down, and now some of my friends are kicking themselves because, you know, £10,000 invested ten years ago is now worth, I am not exaggerating this, almost £1 million.

And these people are kicking themselves, but even after five years when I had proven the concept, by around 1994, the brand hadn't taken off. It took off after that share issue the following year – and I started building a team, I started to have some resources to put into marketing, and it just took off. My sales doubled within a year, and we never looked back. So people didn't necessarily believe in it. In that semi-circle in the Managing Director's office, when I first visited the brewery, I had two people who believed in me. One was the owner of the brewery, the Managing Director of Mysore Breweries in

Bangalore, and the other was the head brewer. Those were the only two people I needed.

Getting close to your customers

Cobra is one of those companies where the enthusiasm is infectious. There is an energy that is noticeable as soon as you enter the building. The company's marketing clearly has much firmer foundations than it did at the start, but I wondered whether any of the marketing principles had changed? Growing organizations often find it challenging to remain as close to their customers as they were when they were small, niche players. I wondered whether this was also true for Cobra. How close is Cobra to its customers today? What steps does the company take to stay in touch?

You were talking earlier about putting your team together and everything I have read about you stresses the importance of the culture of Cobra. How many staff have you currently got working for you?

Well because we outsource just about everything, including all our brewing, we don't count employees in the breweries. If I counted everyone responsible for brewing, as we now have about ten breweries brewing Cobra around the world, we would be talking thousands of people. But our direct employees number about 200.

I get the impression I that you have 200 ambassadors for Cobra beer.

Yes, because everyone is just absolutely proud and passionate about the brand, about the company, about being part of the Cobra team, the Cobra family, and that gives me the most joy. Just seeing how much people have developed here. One employee came to us as a sales rep after we put an ad in the Evening Standard. We didn't even want to hire him at first – he was our third choice for two positions – but he convinced us to give him a chance, and he turned out to be so dedicated and so amazingly hardworking that he's now our Sales Director. Another example is a South African girl who used to deliver sandwiches to our offices. We liked her, so we offered her a part time job in telesales. She rose up the ranks as well, and now she's our HR Manager – our first ever. And she took all the training because that's what she wanted to do, and we supported her through the training because we believed in her. We wanted her to follow her goals. I can give you so many examples of that sort of thing at Cobra, because we work very, very hard to create this environment where you just allow people to flourish, where there are very few rules, where people can come from anywhere and go anywhere, and there are no limits. People are constantly transferring from one area to another, and progressing very rapidly.

How close would you say you are to your customers now, in 2007?

Me as an individual? Well one extreme is that I bumped into Sir Terry Leahy, Tesco's Chief Executive Officer, at a breakaway meeting at the India–UK Investment Summit. He asked me how Tesco was doing with Cobra sales, and I thanked him for being one of our best customers!

That's certainly an opportunity most people don't have!

But of course on the other hand, in the beginning, when we were trying to get a lot of the big distributors to sell our product, it wasn't easy. The word you come across more than anything else in business when you are starting is the word 'no'. Everything is no. One reason is that people don't like change. People are happy with what they've got. In our case, the distributors had their range of products, so why did they need another one? At the distributors, at the restaurant, at the bar, they asked us, 'Why should I take your product? I've got enough. It's just another thing to worry about'. And people will invariably say no. People are resistant to change. And quite often it is because they have got so much on their plate.

The lesson I learned from this is that you have got to be proactive. From the very early days, we decided on a top-down approach. We would get the best Indian restaurants to sell Cobra first, because once the best ones took it we could then go to any of the others and say, well if it's good enough for them then it must be very good. It turned out to be a great strategy, to go for the best first, but not an obvious one because logic would say you work your way *up* to the best.

So we built up to 100 of these top accounts in the London area which we were delivering directly to, and then the distributors started to take an interest in us. They came to us, including the biggest oriental food suppliers in Greater London, which served 1,000 Indian restaurants.

You have got to earn your way through and prove your point by being on the ground. We had to go in and sell to those 100 restaurants, and there were just two of us. We had to organize production in India thousands of miles away, the shipping and distribution from the P&O depot in Canning Town, and releasing the stock from bond. We were always running out of money.

We did the sales as well, phoning the restaurants for their orders each week. And we noticed that if we didn't phone the restaurants for one week, then our sales would just tail off. We would be getting regular re-orders and suddenly we would get no orders, and we'd get a real scare. So we would phone up the restaurants and ask if there was something wrong, because they hadn't ordered the previous week.

And it was because we hadn't phoned them. Sometimes they ran out of Cobra, and had started to sell other beers instead. That's when we realized that your understanding of customers has got to be very deep. You have got to put yourself in their shoes. If you put yourself in the shoes of an owner/manager-run Indian restaurant where you have got a team of six to ten people, where every day you've got fresh food coming in, you've got dozens of suppliers, you've got to go and collect various products, you've got linen, you've got cutlery, you've got crockery, you've got customers coming in through the door, you've got chilled food, you've got frozen food, you've got back of the house, you've got front of the house, you've got to market your restaurant, you've got to do some PR, you've got to recruit … is one brand of beer going to be at the top in your mind? You have got far too much else to deal with.

So if you're not proactive with your customers, regardless of how much they like you and how much they love your product, just the practicalities of life and running a business mean they may not sell your product. It's not their fault. You have *got* to be proactive with your customers.

That sounds like an important lesson for any business. How else did you get close to your customers in the early days?

We would also go to consumer and trade shows. Every time I'm at a show it brings back memories of the trade shows that we used to do. I remember the first stand we ever set up, at the Pub, Club and Leisure Show in Olympia. Our budget was £800 for the stand. We got these cool artists to do some paper backdrops and we made a bar counter out of cases of beer to save costs. We'd be there behind the counters serving and getting close to customers, and we would take every opportunity to get feedback from the customers. We handed out survey forms, which I designed myself, which asked questions such as, 'Is Cobra smoother than any other beer you've drunk?'

Then we would use the statistics from the feedback from those surveys in our trade advertising in magazines. So the headline would read, for example, '95% of customers think that Cobra is the smoothest lager they have ever consumed'.

So even when we couldn't afford focus groups or formalized research, we did this informal research that kept us in touch with the consumers. We would give people a free Cobra pen to fill out the survey. We would encourage them to come back at the end of the day for a free draw for cases of beer, to encourage them to give us feedback. And some of the major decisions in my business have been made on the back of this feedback. One example was when, in 1996, our sales took off after my partner left, and we just had the share issue the year before. Sales doubled in a year, and my production problems nearly quadrupled because the brewery just couldn't cope. So we started to have quality, consistency and availability problems. I was very worried. I had built this brand up as an authentically-imported Indian beer and now the only option I really had was to brew it over here in the UK. But if I did that, would my customers stop drinking my product? I was terrified...

On the other hand, you had built up the brand entirely on the basis of its quality, so you couldn't afford to jeopardize that.

Absolutely. And for a consumer brand, quality is paramount, so I couldn't keep taking the risk, and the problems were getting unmanageable. The volumes had reached hundreds of containers so we were really in a quandary.

That's when I realized what you had to do when you found yourself in a difficult position: you ask the customer. So we had two major consumer shows – one was the BBC Good Food Show, which was one of the biggest food shows, and the other was the Sunday Times Show. One was in London and one was in Birmingham. So we took the opportunity, and I slipped in an additional question in the surveys that we handed out. We listed four factors about Cobra beer, and we asked customers to rank them in order of importance. The four factors were:

(1) that it is a premium lager;
(2) that it is brewed to an authentic Indian recipe;
(3) that it is imported from India;
(4) its extra-smooth, less gassy taste.

We asked thousands of consumers in both London and Birmingham at these two top shows. When we analysed the results, we couldn't believe it. The most important factor, by a wide margin, was the extra-smooth, less gassy taste. The least important factor, by an equally wide margin, was that it was imported from India.

I never looked back, and I was able to brew beer in England when I started with the Charles Wells brewery in Bedford. It seemed right. Born in Bangalore, brewed in Bedford. We started manufacturing here in Britain in 1997, and instantly we had world-class quality and world-class packaging. All my problems switched off, world-class quality at my doorstep switched on. And again, it was the customer who gave me the confidence to do that.

And when you go to these trade shows now, are you still running surveys and getting feedback?

Always, always, and of course now we have the added advantage of also being able to do all the focus groups and all the research.

So how would you know if consumer drinking tastes were changing? How quickly would you know if there was a trend towards a different type of beer, or even towards, say, an alternative to beer when drinking with food?. How quickly would you pick up on that trend?

You are watching the market the whole time and again, as your company grows bigger, it is about communication, and constantly getting that feedback through and making sure that not only are your messages getting out, but you are constantly getting messages back in. You do that through a number of mechanisms. For example, if I am in the country and in the office on a Friday evening, I will just gather together whoever is in the office. So if we've had a monthly meeting it might be more than 100 people who come down from different parts of the country, or on a normal Friday at least 60 or 70 people. We just gather round and I tell them a few things that I've been up to, ask if any members of the management team have anything to report, and people talk about new developments. We just share what is happening in the marketplace – what our customers are saying, what people's friends are saying – in an informal manner, for about 15 or 20 minutes just gathered around.

On the other hand, once a month we have a formal communications meeting when presentations are made by each of the teams. These usually include PowerPoint presentations and training. So we have a formal mechanism as well. A member of our marketing team is also constantly tracking what the competition is doing, and what's happening in the industry, and actually keeps the whole company updated with regular reports.

Then, every week the management team meets. Now historically that management team has been the Finance Director, two Sales Directors, the Marketing Director, the Financial Controller and I. I suddenly realized that as we were growing, what we actually needed was a weekly meeting of *all* the management, not just the top team. So we widened it, and now those meetings include all the different sales managers and the marketing manager. By widening that net, suddenly the communication and the feedback you are getting is much better. So it is constantly evolving, but again it is driven by communication, information, customers.

In terms of communication with customers, could Cobra be any closer to its customers?

You can always be closer. I mean, we take every opportunity we can to try to get closer to our customers. For example, we founded the trade magazine 'Tandoori' – I am no longer involved with Tandoori but I was one of its founders and its publisher. I realized then that I needed to reach out to these Indian restaurants that were scattered all around the country. There are very few chains of Indian restaurants – the largest chain of Indian restaurants today is about 20, out of 10,000 Indian restaurants. Of course, at the time I started Cobra I was in a growing market, and not only with lager. All the odds were against me but I had two factors in my favour: one was lager and the other was Indian restaurants. In rough terms, there was just a handful of Indian restaurants in the fifties, which went up to 3,000 by 1980, 6,000 by 1990, and just over 10,000 today. And of course it is thanks to Indian restaurants that Indian food is part of the British way of life – we are a nation of curryholics, addicted to Indian food emotionally and physically. People cook Indian food at home, buy it chilled from the supermarket as well as from Indian restaurants, and it is all thanks to the Indian restaurants it happened. So I knew I was in a growing market there as well.

I realized that I didn't have a sales force that could reach out to all these restaurants around the country and I looked around for a trade magazine that went out on a regular basis to these restaurants. There wasn't any such thing, so I started one, and Tandoori to this day is the leading trade magazine to the whole sector and all other beers have been able to advertise in it.

Tandoori has all relevant information and news for the restaurants, and it's a great read – it is useful to the whole industry, and it started off by turning the frustration of not being able to communicate with restaurants into an opportunity. The mail-shots I used to send out to restaurants were very expensive, very time-consuming, and on the whole very ineffective because most mail-shots go straight into the bin. And here was a way of actually communicating with the restaurants on a regular basis. We still do it to this day, even though I have no ownership of Tandoori. I haven't done for a few years, but we are the biggest advertiser.

You can always try to communicate with your industry, and with your customers, better. We had a huge supermarket promotion where you could win Sony Bravia TVs. People had to enter via our website. Through that we have built up a database of 70,000 to 80,000 consumers. It is brilliant because it lets you know where they bought it, whether it was a four pack of non-alcoholic, a four-pack of Lower Cal, or a four-pack of normal Cobra. So you can even see what people are buying. Through that promotion, we've built an email list of about 40,000 customers, and we're just about to start a regular email newsletter.

Innovation

Karan Bilimoria had outlined very clearly that he had known all along the strategy that would enable him to establish Cobra as a global beer brand in a highly competitive marketplace. Yet so much has changed in the 17 years that Cobra has been around. Who could have predicted, for example, that email would transform the way that Cobra communicates with its customers and consumers? How important is adapting to changing technology for Cobra?

You have to adapt to changing technology. It is about always being close to your customer, communicating with your customer. It's about non-stop innovation. Restless creativity. Restless innovation.

Take the embossed icons on our bottles, for example. For the first time, a consumer brand was telling its story visually as part of the packaging. Not just a pretty bottle, but a reason for doing it. And again, from where the customer is concerned, it's interesting. They want to know what the icons represent. And then they discover that they tell the Cobra story, each one portraying a stage in the Cobra Beer story. So we are entertaining our customers the whole time.

Then there's our CobraVision short film competition on television, which we run in conjunction with itv2, itv3 and itv4 movies. It's the first time in the world that the idents which are sponsoring the programme are a film competition, and the idents are films submitted by the public. Those five-second films were all submitted by the public. CobraVision is about young film-makers showing their films on national TV. Each one of those five-second films goes into a competition – the CobraVision Awards – so these filmmakers, predominantly young filmmakers, not only get their films shown on national TV with viewers of between 500,000 and 1 million per evening, but they also get entered into a competition. We held our first ever CobraVision awards at the Curzon Mayfair cinema, and we had Oscar nominees, senior people in the film industry as judges. When I saw the winners on the stage last year, what gave me huge satisfaction was seeing predominantly young British filmmakers. You are encouraging the British film industry, you are encouraging creativity, you are entertaining your viewers and your consumers, because they don't know what is coming up next. It is so creative; it's not the same jingle, the same old product shot before and after each commercial break. It's a different way of doing things entirely.

You mentioned the need for constant innovation. Is that the factor that nurtures the loyalty to Cobra that your customers clearly have?

What we noticed right at the beginning, very early on, was that the Cobra brand was spreading by word of mouth. People would discover it at the restaurant, then they would tell their family, they would tell their friends. We couldn't afford mainstream advertising for the first eight years, until we ran a campaign with Saatchi & Saatchi in 1998. The first time we even did any television or cinema advertising was in 2003, 13 years after we started, because that was the first time we could afford it. At the end of 2006, however, we ran a new ad campaign and we were the biggest televised beer brand on British television, just three years after our first television advertisement.

But when we started, our only form of marketing was that one flimsy table card. We couldn't even afford glasses. But by starting from the grass roots, which builds up a following, it becomes almost a sort of cult. And people just take ownership of it: they discovered it, they tell people about it – and it has got to be a product that is genuinely special and different for you to be able to do that. The product substantively has to stand up, and that's what Cobra has always done. From day one we got a100 per cent reorder rate. When the restaurant owners gave us that chance, then our product had to deliver.

The challenge for a brand that has grown from the grassroots comes when you start mainstream advertising. You don't want to alienate those people who have taken you to where you are now; in other words, the customers who really believed in your product. So if you commercialize the brand, you risk losing those foundation customers who helped you to grow. So we have been very careful.

In every new campaign, I am there at the meetings for its development. For the recent campaign on television, I was there at every meeting, and when we made decisions as to what to do, I threw it back to the drawing board three times before we got to where we wanted. It's about really working closely with your agency. You have to question, is our communication in keeping with the Cobra brand? Is it quirky, has it got that wit, humour, is it clever? Is it all those things? The strap line now is: 'Cobra: Unusual thing, excellence'. You wouldn't believe the amount of work we put into that! It's a three-dimensional line – 'Unusual thing, excellence' – because excellence is unusual, Cobra is unusual and Cobra is excellent. It works.

Going against the grain

A lot of it is also zigging when people are zagging. You are going against the grain a lot of the time. It is almost a contradiction. You must be customer-driven. In everything I have said you will see that the customer is at the heart of it. You are close to the customer, you are communicating with the customer, you are listening to the customer, you are consulting the customer, you are asking the customer – and of course, you were originally a customer yourself. So if you actually think about it, everything starts from being a customer.

So in what way would you say are you going against the grain?

Often in what you are doing, you are, as an entrepreneur, presenting something that doesn't already exist, or it exists in a different format from the one that people are used to, and you are asking them to accept change. So the paradox is that you are giving customers what they want, but the customers don't even know they want it because it doesn't exist!

Let me illustrate. Why is it that in an industry that is centuries-old, no one thought of a less gassy, extra-smooth lager that would appeal to ale drinkers, and that would go well with spicy food? No one had done that before. So you are asking customers to accept something that they don't know about. It's like that classic quote from Henry Ford, regarding the first car he ever built: 'If I had asked my customers what they wanted, they would have said a faster horse.' That quote sums up exactly what I'm talking about.

Another example I will give you is with our new product development. Take the non-alcoholic Cobra. Now that is a very simple example of my hating every single non-alcoholic beer I have ever drunk. So I set out to find one that was reasonably drinkable. I found its producer, I discovered that it had special technology that used special yeast and actually brewed it like real beer, and then we combined it with our hops and brewed it in two countries, in Holland and Poland, and produced the best tasting alcohol-free beer ever. It's an alcohol-free beer that is actually really drinkable. It's simple.

Then there's our low-calorie beer. Lots of drinks companies have produced 'light' beers. But what are they? They're certainly light on taste! But are they low-calorie? Sometimes. Low-carbohydrate? Sometimes. Low-alcohol? Sometimes. It's all very confusing. So we just set out to produce a low-calorie beer, with fewer than 100 calories a bottle, which is low-carbohydrate and really drinkable.

But the one that was really a ground-breaking innovation for us was King Cobra, in the champagne bottles. Now that stemmed from developing a strong lager for India. We did the development work with our Belgian brew master, Koen Cruycke, and our British production director, Robert Knox. You have to have the best people, and we have the best. Robert Knox has brewed in 20 countries around the world, and he is one of the best brewers in the world.

So in developing King Cobra, Koen came up with this terrific 8 per cent strength beer. It was basically a Cobra brewed to a higher strength. And we did trial after trial, and we came up with the right taste, because the challenge with strong beers is they can be very syrupy and very sweet and not nice to drink. What happens is that people compensate for the syrupiness and sweetness by making them overly bitter. You try the strong lagers – I can't mention any brands, but they are disgusting. So we set out to produce one that was delicious. And I decided that I wanted to release that strong beer here in the UK. Of course, the problem with strong beers over here is that the connotation is not good, because of the park-bencher stereotype of people who drink strong lagers. But on the other hand, I have tasted and enjoy to this day delicious Belgian beers that are 8 per cent strength, but they are not technically lagers. My whole management team was trying to dissuade me from doing it here, because of the image of strong lagers.

But I was talking about taking this to a different level, and actually producing one that is so drinkable and enjoyable that anyone will enjoy drinking it because it will be such high quality, in the same way they enjoy drinking these Belgian beers. So Koen, who is Belgian, pointed out that they have double-fermented ales in Belgium but no one has ever tried the double fermentation process with a lager. He asked if I would like him to experiment. So, of course, I said that he should go for it! He experimented and immediately after the first trial we thought that we had brewed the best ever strong lager. There were so many extra textures and aromas.

Then he asked to take it one step further. He suggested that we should brew it in Poland, chill it after it has finished brewing, and take it at four degrees centigrade in tankers to Belgium. Then at Rodenbach, one of the most famous old Belgian trappist breweries, we would put it into champagne bottles, add an extra Belgian lambic ale yeast into the lager, seal the bottles, and, like champagne, let it double ferment in the bottles in the cellars. We would raise the temperature up to 25 degrees so the secondary fermentation starts in the bottle and then, unlike champagne where they freeze it and then they take out the yeast, here we would let the yeast settle as a sediment in the bottle. We would cool it down, and then we would have an un-pasteurized beer in champagne bottles. The world's first double-fermented lager – King Cobra. It is such an outstanding beer, but why did it take a small British company like ours, a beer of Indian origin, made in Poland and in Belgium, to create the world's first double-fermented lager?

So the picture I am getting is that you should get as close to your customer as you can, but the Henry Ford example, the King Cobra example, often means that your solution is not a solution to a problem that customers have identified for themselves.

Absolutely. CobraVision – a film competition open to the public. Embossed bottles – for the first time in history a consumer brand telling a story visually as part of the packaging. So it is constantly doing things that no one has done before.

And could your marketing principles, and your approach to your customers, apply and work in any sector with any product?

I have this firm belief that, where sales are concerned, you have to get to know the product you are selling, and you have got to believe in it, otherwise you are a con-man. But I do believe if you can sell a bottle of beer, you can sell a jumbo jet.

Determination and destination: learning to 'never give up'

Karan Bilimoria is clearly not someone who gives something a try, yet moves on if it doesn't work out as expected. Yet there must have been times when Cobra looked like a hopeless cause. I was building a list of qualities that might be needed for the founder of a venture like Cobra, and determination was high up on it.

So the belief has to be there, the quality has to be there, the passion has to be there, the determination, the knocking on doors ...

And that determination goes right through. People ask me if I ever thought of giving up, and yes, you run out of money all the time, you are down in the dumps, but you never think of giving up.

Back at the beginning we ran Cobra from our home, and the dining room and sitting room were our office. The dining room table was our office table. My business partner, my wife and I all shared the same house. We roughed it for years. It was really hard. That's the other thing: there is no shortcut. When I was driving around in my 2CV, my contemporaries were with the Goldman Sachs of this world earning, even in those days, hundreds of thousands of pounds.

But you were on a journey, and you knew where the end point was, and nothing was going to stop you getting there?

Well that's another point I want to make: success is not a destination, it's a journey. There isn't an end point.

But going back to the hard times. We had run out of money again, and I remember taking my wallet out and finding that all I had was pennies in it. All our credit cards were up to their limits, all our bank cards were over their limits. Do you feel down in the dumps? You bet you do. Do you feel like giving up? Never! You wake up the next morning and you find a way out of it. That saying of Churchill's – 'never, never, never, never give up' – is my favourite, favourite saying.

So do you ever get frustrated that the journey is ongoing and that there is no destination?

Not at all, because you have always got new challenges. For me now the huge excitement is India. Again, this is talking about customers. If you look at the bigger picture, and I believe a lot of management and leadership is the ability to take the very big view, our 'Grand Canyon plan' is about looking ahead at a billion dollar brand, and thinking about where we are going to be selling it and how. It's called the 'Grand Canyon plan' because I was actually flying over the Grand Canyon when I sketched it!

So I am always thinking ahead, always thinking about the long-term. Before I shipped out the first container of beer from India I went to the computer room in the brewery – we didn't have PCs in those days – and I did a Lotus 1-2-3 schedule, month-by-month, container-by-container for five years. And I had never sold a bottle of beer in my life. So there is an element of always taking that big view but also being able to drill down right to the smallest detail when required – a combination of being able to do both those is important, I think.

And so the accountancy training was absolutely vital?

Well it was useful, there is no question about it. I mean, to be able to read balance sheets in your sleep is pretty handy! There is no question it is very useful.

If I can just return to the Grand Canyon plan: in India today, per capita beer consumption isn't even 0.7 litres per person per year. The world's highest beer consumption is in the Czech Republic, at around 160 litres per person per year – it's around 100 here in Britain. Now I'm not saying India is ever going to become a Czech Republic or a UK, but China is a fair comparison. China started its economic reform in 1978. They made a deliberate decision that if people are going to drink, they would rather they drank beer. They freed up beer production and availability. The Chinese beer market was at 0.6 litres per person per year in 1978, and in 25 years, by 2003, China overtook the United States as the biggest beer market in the world by volume.

Now India is a beer market that is growing ahead of the GDP growth. It is growing about 10 per cent year-on-year. India has a population where over 50 per cent of the population is under the age of 20. It is getting more and more global and outward-looking as a country and as an economy. It is a young country, and the climate, the conditions, the fact that prohibition has failed wherever it has been implemented – everything indicates that and in the future beer is the ideal, ideal drink for India. I believe the Indian beer market is just catching up with China, and if the Indian market grows like China then you're looking at the Indian beer market growing by 30 to 40 times in the next 20 to 25 years. And we've only just started there.

And you have created a brand that the Indians are waiting for!

Yes! The wonderful thing is, in India they see it as their own beer that's done well abroad, and they also see it in a way as a foreign beer. It is almost like the non-resident Indian who has returned.

Conclusions and recommendations

Lord Karan Bilimoria challenges every assumption you will ever make about entrepreneurs, and how to establish and grow a successful business. Meeting him was an unforgettable and unique experience. I know other people who are passionate about what they do. I've spent time with people who are focused, motivated, even driven. Occasionally, I have met people with all of these qualities. That's only part of the picture, though. Karan Bilimoria is certainly all of these things. But he is also gentle, calm and absolutely charming. He went out of his way to make me welcome, comfortable and fed. He insisted, for example, on sending out for a salad and sandwich to keep me going. And no visitor, he told me, leaves the Cobra headquarters without a heavy carrier bag full of beer, and I was no exception. In short, he is absolutely delightful company.

Nothing illustrates his calmness better than his role as one of the panel of judges on Sky TV's 'The Big Idea', partnering Ruth Badger and Craig Johnston. Where his colleagues shouted their support, or otherwise, for their chosen entrepreneurs, Karan calmly and gently considered ideas on the basis of the ideas' merits and the passion of the people behind them. It was fascinating television.

The formula of converting dissatisfaction with a product or service into a successful business has clearly worked for Cobra Beer. I still regard the launch of Cobra, however, as a world apart from the approach that agencies, books and courses use to teach people how to start up in business. Karan mentioned that his idea would have been laughed at by an organization like management consulting firm McKinsey, so he never approached them. On the BBC's 'Dragons' Den' television programme, the investors look at the experience of the management team, the sales they have already made, and the feasibility of the forecasts they are predicting. Karan Bilimoria certainly undertook exhaustive research, but it was research to find the perfect recipe, the optimum brewing technique, the most talented brewer to work with. When I questioned him about how thoroughly he had researched his marketplace, he answered that he 'knew his ale-loving friends would hate lager' and that he 'saw people struggling in Indian restaurants'. The fact is, he was absolutely right.

I suspect that the explanation rests with his belief that to be successful, you must be prepared to 'go against the grain', and to 'zig rather than zag'. Sometimes, in your efforts to meet your customers' needs, you have to accept that they may not know what their needs are. They may not have appreciated that what they wanted was a less gassy, premium lager, brewed to appeal to ale and lager drinkers alike. Certainly, no brewer had considered the concept before Cobra. Zigging can be dangerous, however. It takes confidence, and a lot of guts, to choose to sell your beer in bottles big enough to share, when your customers are telling you that they want small bottles.

So what else defines Karan Bilimoria's leadership style? For a start, he's not afraid to recruit the very best people for the job. Being upstaged has clearly not crossed his mind. Finding the best brewer in the world clearly has. The drive for 'restless creativity' and 'restless innovation' is also significant. No one

Managing customer needs checklist

If you are thinking about how better to manage your customers' needs, here are some issues to think about. You might want to find a few, valuable minutes to take a clean sheet of paper and jot down any ideas that the following list generates.

Market and customer research

What are you doing differently, or better, than your competitors? What could you be doing even better? Do your sales skills need a makeover? What mechanisms do you have in place for 'spotting a gap in the market and a market in the gap'?

Consumer testing

How often do you talk to your customers about what they like, and don't like, about your products and services? Do you listen to what they say? What action have you taken as a result? Can you honestly say that you 'never, ever go forward without checking it with the consumer'?

Kowing who your customers are

How well can you define who your customers actually are? Are your customers different from the end users of your product? Who do you market and sell to? What measures are in place to communicate with both groups? Do you have a long-term 'game plan' and are your customers part of it?

Credibility gap

Are you passionate about what you do? Does this come across to those around you? Are you confident in your products and services? Do you believe in them? Do people have confidence in you?

Getting close to your customers

Are your team members and colleagues ambassadors for your organization? Would you feel confident if they met and spoke with your customers? Have you assembled the best possible team that you could? As your organization grows, are you still as close to your customers as you once were?

Innovation

Can you think of examples where you have deliberately gone 'against the grain'? Do you struggle with the concept that you are meeting your customers' needs, but that they may not know what their needs are? Can you and do you 'zig' when those around you 'zag'?

Determination

Are you tempted to give up? Do you tend to see things through? Where are you on your journey?

Sir Digby Jones on managing information and knowledge

Sir Digby Jones, Former Director-General of the CBI, Senior Advisor to the Executive of Deloitte, Senior Advisor to Barclays Capital, Special Advisor to Ford of Europe

'If I could give someone three things to succeed in twenty-first century Britain, the first one would be the use of your memory and the ability to handle knowledge – to handle the information that comes in, to remember things, to discard stuff and to exploit stuff … The second thing would be confidence … And the third thing, and there is no escape from this: you work very hard and there is no substitute for this.'

Born in Birmingham on 28 October 1955, Sir Digby Jones began his schooldays at Alvechurch Primary School Birmingham (1960–1966) before winning a major scholarship to Bromsgrove School (1966–1974). He gained an Upper Second class Honours Degree in Law at University College London in 1977.

He was awarded a University Cadetship in the Royal Navy (1974–1977) then took articles with the Birmingham corporate law firm Edge & Ellison in 1978. He was admitted as a Solicitor in 1980.

He made Partner at Edge & Ellison in 1984 and it was in corporate finance and client development that he made his name. He was responsible for developing the firm's London presence and establishing its representation in many European countries and several states in America. He was involved in most of the major management buy-outs and merger and acquisition activity in the West Midlands in the late 1980s and early 1990s.

He was made Deputy Senior Partner in 1990 and Senior Partner in 1995.

In 1998 he joined KPMG as vice chairman of Corporate Finance, acting as close adviser to many public companies across the United Kingdom and in KPMG's global markets.

Sir Digby served as Director-General of the CBI, the Confederation of British Industry, the UK's 'Voice of Business', from 1 January 2000 to 30 June 2006 where he regularly visited businesses in the UK and worldwide – taking their views back to those who make the rules. During his appointment he took the British business message to 70 different countries. He met on a regular basis political, business and media figures in the UK and around the world.

He holds a number of senior corporate advisory positions. Senior Advisor to the Executive of Deloitte; Senior Advisor to Barclays Capital; Corporate and Governmental Affairs Advisor to Ford of Europe and its Premier Automotive Group; Senior Advisor to JCB; Special Advisor to His Royal Highness the Duke of York in connection with his role as the UK Special Representative for International Trade and Investment; Senior Advisor to Monitise Ltd; Corporate Affairs advisor to Bucknall Austin Ltd; Member of the Advisory Board of Thales (UK) Ltd; Non-Executive Director of Alba plc, i-Clean Systems Ltd. and Leicester Tigers Rugby plc.

He serves as the UK's Skills Envoy, campaigning for both private and public sector employers to raise the level of skills of all of their employees to Level Two by 2010.

Sir Digby is a Fellow of University College London (2004), an Honorary Fellow of Cardiff University (2004), an Honorary Doctor of the University of Central England (2002), the University of Birmingham (2002), the University of Manchester, Institute of

Science and Technology (2003), the University of Hertfordshire (2004), Middlesex University (2005), Sheffield Hallam University (2005), Aston University (2006), the University of Hull (2006), Queen's University, Belfast (2006), Warwick University (2006), Bradford University (2006), Thames Valley University (2006) and Wolverhampton University (2006). He is President of the University College, London Campaign, a visiting professor at the University of Hull Business School and Chairman of the Birmingham University Business School Advisory Board.

He is Chairman of the Cancer Research UK Corporate Ambassadors and Chairman of the Corporate Development Board of Sense, helping those born deaf and blind. He is also a Fellow of UNICEF. He serves as an Ambassador for Investors in People. He is President of the Diversity Works initiative – a programme led by the disability organization Scope, a Diamond Ambassador for Mencap's WorkRight initiative, designed to spread the message of equality for disabled people, a Vice-President of Birmingham Hospice, a Patron of Lifecycle UK, a patron of Where Next? dedicated to helping autistic young people achieve fulfilling employoment, a Patron of the Campaign for Learning, a Patron of Every Child a Reader, a Patron of London Excellence, a Corporate Ambassador and member of the Royal British Legion, a member of the Aston Reinvestment Trust, a member of the City of Birmingham Symphony Orchestra Development Trust, Director of the Birmingham Hippodrome Theatre, and a Vice President of the Friends of the British Library.

Sir Digby is President of the Ambassadors for the West Midlands region, Vice President of the Birmingham Civic Society, President of Birmingham Forward, the professional services lobby group and Patron of the World Class Stratford-Upon-Avon initiative. He is a member of the Yorkshire Society, a Freeman of the City of London, a member of the Japan Society and an Honorary Fellow of the Institution of Mechanical Engineers.

In 1998, as Chairman of the Birmingham Hospice Appeal, which raised £1.5 million, he personally raised £218,000 towards their target by cycling from John O'Groats to Land's End in 14 days. He ran the 2005 London Marathon in under six hours raising £191,000 for both Cancer Research UK and UNICEF.

He appears regularly on television, radio and in the newspapers, being known for his firm views on several aspects of life in a globalized economy. He is an active public speaker at events and engagements all over the world.

He was appointed a Knight Bachelor in the 2005 New Year Honours' List.

Sir Digby is married to Pat. They live in Marylebone and Warwickshire. He enjoys the theatre, skiing, football, rugby and cricket and has more than a passing interest in military history.

I had prepared for my meeting with Sir Digby Jones by researching and reading a range of interviews he had given with national and regional newspapers during his tenure as Director-General of the CBI. Whilst these made very interesting reading, they didn't provide the preparation I had hoped for. Described as 'like a very cuddly boxer' by The Sunday Telegraph, and 'less Billy Bunter and more John Bull' by Scotland on Sunday, I desperately tried to build a mental picture of 'one of the most recognisable business faces in Britain'.

However, the more I read, the more reassured I felt. I felt heartened to learn that we shared the same opinion about the BBC television programme 'The Apprentice'. In an interview with The Sunday Times, he said: 'It puts business in a very bad light. Young people will be turned off because they think they will be shouted at by a horrible, fat, old, rich bloke.'

Hardly one to mince his words, I was confident that if I asked straight questions, he would reward me with straight answers. It was a fantastic opportunity for me, but I was a little worried that I was discussing the subject of managing information and knowledge with him. Would he be stimulated by the subject matter? Would he have enough to say? Would we just spend an hour or two discussing IT systems?

In my mind, there were several issues that I think affect British business that I wanted to hear Sir Digby's opinion on. No one would deny that the amount of information passing an individual's desk each day has grown dramatically in recent years. What techniques or methods would he recommend for handling and managing information? For someone who has always been out and about, how has he personally managed to stay on top of the information he is required to absorb? Perhaps the two most important issues were about sharing knowledge *between individuals and teams within an organization, and also protecting that knowledge, and turning it into intellectual property.*

I thought I would begin by asking him whether he recognized the Chartered Management Institute's quotation that, 'the amount of information produced and used by individuals and organizations continues to grow'.

The impact of the knowledge economy

I wanted to begin with a quotation from the Chartered Management Institute which says that, 'the amounts of information produced and used by individuals and organisations continues to grow'. Is that something you agree with?

Yes. It's on two levels, isn't it? Britain has made this shift with a considerable amount of pain and angst, and the journey is not finished by any means, but we are way ahead of any other country in Europe on this – I actually think we are ahead of America in this. We have made this shift towards a value-added, innovative, branded, quality economy for goods and services. We don't protect our markets, we don't put up tariffs and subsidies, we don't indulge in the hypocrisy of France and America, we just get on with it and we have restructured our economy. So that's why we don't dig coal out of the ground any more, that's why we don't make commodity steel, that's why we have the greatest and best financial services industry on earth. The reason is that we have moved to a value-added, innovative economy. You are always going to need people to do manual work; pick the fruit off the fields, do the labour on the building site, wait at table, chambermaids in hotels, all that sort of stuff, of course you are. But there are going to be no sustainable jobs for people without a skill of some sort within the next five years.

So the need for knowledge, the acquisition of knowledge, the handling of knowledge, the transmission of knowledge and information and the application of that to the wealth-creation process has never been more important and is an ongoing dynamic. Now at that level we are doing better than I think we ever thought we could. Of course, the big thing about a service-based economy is that it uses people. So we have got a low level of unemployment. We have got a hell of a lot of people who don't earn a lot of money, but they are in work. Those self-same people in Germany and France are part of their 11 or 12 per cent unemployment, and in France in the under 25s it is about 22 per cent, and this is because they haven't made this transition. So they haven't got this service-based economy where these people will work, albeit for low wages. So when people or trade unions say, we're a low paid economy – oh fine but they are in work. If they don't want them to have a job, albeit lowly paid, well no problem, we will go and do it in China. It's a shame they don't campaign for skills in the way they fight to keep yesterday's jobs.

So that is the one part of our knowledge. The other part is that the whole electronization of our lives is predicated on the handling, transmission and acquisition of knowledge and information. Everything from the Internet to the mobile phone – the whole thing is predicated on that.

The impression I get from what you are saying is that the inevitable result in the transition is a

swamping of knowledge for workers at all levels, as well as for managers and directors.

Oh yes. The upside of it is that without it we are dead. We are a globally engaged country, we trade like crazy, we are number one or two in the world in aviation, we are number one or two in the world in financial services, number one or two in the world in academia and pharmaceuticals. We are a class act , and we are still home to more different car makers than anywhere else on earth. Formula One employs 50,000 people in Britain, you know. Engineering, motor car engineering – top of the gang. Now all that stuff we are very, very good at. Creative industries – about 12 per cent of the world's creative industry's GDP we do in this country – art, video, advertising, design, architecture, music, film, all of those things.

What have I just described to you, if it's not the handling of information and knowledge? The downside – and this is, I think, one of the great challenges for managers, and a huge challenge in the public and private sectors at management level – is that there is *too much* information, and how do you sift it, how do you prioritize it, how do you become good at picking out the stuff you need and discarding the stuff you don't? How are you going to be skilled at prioritizing? How do you handle the swamp, which can really depress people and move pressure to stress very quickly? How do you educate people to handle information better so they don't waste people's time with giving them too much information or unnecessary information? And then at the same time, there are two great things that authority does – be it regulators, be it for this purpose media, I mean anybody with a degree of influence and authority. First, they say, 'Right, you cc Fred on every email, so Fred is now deemed to have seen it, so if Fred does nothing about it and the shit hits the fan in five years' time well, you knew about it Fred'. So what do you do about that? Second, you have the whole issue of regulation and regulatory form-filling. Just try being a police officer trying to make an arrest ... or a chief executive of a hospital.

The whole red tape issue.

The whole red tape issue is born out of enhanced information and a greater knowledge transfer. The ability to store it, the ability to deal with it, it is all born out of that, because it is easier to do, far more easy than it used to be.

Stress, pressure and the impact on individuals

Sir Digby Jones had highlighted several concerns that I wanted to investigate further. He had talked about the impact that IT has had on individuals, particularly in terms of the amount of information that has resulted. It might be convenient to copy a number of people in on emails, but the swamp of information that results is a concern. Then there is the issue of red tape. The notion is that regulation and form-filling has evolved because, with IT systems in place, it is so much easier to store the information, so you might as well collect it.

I wanted to ask Sir Digby his views on two separate, but related, concerns. First, I wanted to discuss the effect that the increase in information and knowledge has had on the average British worker. Does this increase explain the growing levels of stress and pressure in the British workforce and, if so, what is to be done about it? Second, for someone who, as Director-General of the CBI, was expected to have an incisive and up-to-date comment on just about anything, how does he decide what information is important and what is not? How does he prioritize his agenda? How does he keep on top?

As Director-General of the CBI, you always gave the impression in interviews, or when writing for newspapers, that you had a comment to make on virtually anything of value or noteworthy to business – and yet, by your own admission, you are always out visiting business, you are always travelling about. How do you personally decide what is relevant or important, and what is not?

Three things. One is, I delegate. I am a very, very good delegator. I do not employ clever people to work for and with me and then do the job myself. I have no problem in trusting them. Sometimes, being human, they let me down. But frankly you've got to trust them. And you give them the appropriate praise: if it is their idea or their piece of work, then you tell whoever reads it that it's their piece of work, and you surround yourself with clever people. So they then start being the interface for handling a lot of that information. For example, they sift my emails. When I first got the job seven years ago I did a speech in a hotel in Manchester and I was then in my hotel room and doing my emails on my laptop at two in the morning. It was ridiculous! So I said that's it, you guys can sift it, you can sort it, and you give me what is important so I can read it, and you deal with the rest. That system works. Was it 100 per cent foolproof? No. Am I prepared to carry the can if they let me down which in turn means that I've let somebody down? Yes, of course I am. That's why I'm paid to be the boss and that's why I'm appointed as the boss.

The second thing I do is, I read – I read prodigiously. I get driven around, I sit on airplanes, I sit on trains and I read. I read the *Times* and the *Financial Times* every day, the *Sunday Times* and the *Observer* on a Sunday – and as I go to bed at night, well thank God for satellite news and News24 or Sky News, every time of day or night I've got it, which is fabulous. When I am overseas I watch BBC World. I don't watch CNN because I don't want to know only what is happening in America, I want to know what is happening in the world through independent eyes! So I keep absolutely up to date on that.

Then the third thing is, and I am quite good at this, I am a ruthless prioritizer.

So the typical very well-rehearsed model of urgency and importance – if it's not urgent, or not important, it just gets chucked away?

Or it certainly waits its turn. I am very ruthless at managing myself.

Are you a speed reader?

Yes – and I have a very good memory.

Short- and long-term?

Yes. But I am not particularly IT-literate. I don't have a computer at all. I haven't got one at home. Pat and I do not have a computer in the house. I haven't got a laptop. I am a prodigious texter and a big user of mobiles, but I don't have a computer. Matt and Aimée are my two PAs – Matt's at Deloitte and Aimée is at BARCAP – and they do the lot. If you email me, it goes to Matt. I know how to use a computer, but I just don't have one. I go on the web by saying, 'Matt, go on the web'. Aimée does my research and project work.

So if you are in a hotel and there is a paper that Matt thinks you ought to read …

He faxes it to me.

I'd like to come back to that, because I'd like to look at the impact that has on the stress and balance and staying in control.

I do take my holidays. I have six weeks' holiday a year and I always, always take them. I have taken them all through Edge & Ellison, all through KPMG, all through the CBI and now I still always take my holidays. In the CBI I probably rang in once a week and said, 'Is everything OK?', but I had a deputy – John Cridland – who was really good. And why do it myself on holiday if I have a damn good deputy?

It's the management of yourself, that's what's so important. Although I don't often work on Saturdays I do sometimes work for two or three hours on Sundays, in the afternoon or evening. For example, last night – I had a whole pile of work to do. Now because I'm a human being I found myself starting to do the easy things first. I even did some things which actually were not time-critical for today at all, but they were easy, so I had to force myself to move on to the more challenging things, which were

time-critical for today. Handling the information is very important. If I have one problem with this, it is that I find it very difficult to say no. I'm not good at saying no – I like pleasing people and I like doing things for people.

And is it one of your PA Matt's roles ...

To rein me in? Yes! And he does as well.

You talk about having a good memory. Is that something you've always had or you've learned?

No I've always had it. For instance, I don't use notes when I speak. People say, oh it comes easy for you – it doesn't. I always get nervous before I speak, but I excuse myself over the coffee and I will go and sit in the loo, put the lid down and just for five minutes get my act together and just think, 'That's the order in which I want to talk about it, those are the facts I want to bring into it, that's where I want to leave the audience at the end of it'. I plan it every time. So although it looks like I just stand up and do it off the cuff, it's actually planned. But if it wasn't for my memory, I wouldn't be able to do that.

If I could give someone three things to succeed in twenty-first century Britain, the first one would be the use of your memory and the ability to handle knowledge – to handle the information that comes in, to remember things, to discard stuff and to exploit stuff.

So the first ingredient of success is a combination of prioritizing and memory?

Yes, prioritizing and memory, and the discipline of giving yourself time to do it.

The second thing would be confidence. But that comes with knowing you are feeling competent about what you are doing. You are then confident, and feel on top. You may be under pressure, but you are not under stress. Stress is pressure you cannot deal with. I will come back to that.

And the third thing, and there is no escape from this: you work very hard and there is no substitute for this. Twenty-first century developed economies face huge challenges and you can't escape the work ethic, full stop. It doesn't mean that you don't make time to go and see your kid at his speech day, it doesn't mean that you don't get home and take your wife to the theatre – it is just a question of handling your time and working hard.

It sounds to me, from what you are saying, as if you don't suffer stress because you have got the balance between work and your life outside work?

Yes. I'll give you an example. Pat and I have just been away for a month. Between the two jobs, I did a month of quite a lot of speeches and TV and other things, I did a month of being briefed on all these jobs I'm now doing, and then I had a month off, and we went away on a three-week cruise around the Black Sea and then a week in Australia. We got back last Monday. And I'm a big 'Spooks' fan – and I taped those four episodes for the four weeks that I missed. And yesterday I said to Pat, 'I am going to curl up on the sofa and I'm going to watch all four!' Now, I've got a whole pile of work to do and I've got calls to return and all sorts, but I promised myself I was going to do it, and my time is important to me, and *I* matter to me. So I did it.

You see, many people say, 'I haven't got time to do that because I've got to do all this work'. Well fine, but you must put some balance in your life. Pressure is fine, stress is not. I know what stress is like. I can remember in 1997 I was senior partner of the law firm Edge & Ellison, and I had a great time, loved it and all that, I was very young to be doing the job and I wanted the firm to go down a particular path, and frankly they wouldn't. I tried to cajole them, I tried to push them, and at the end of the day the only thing I was left with was saying, 'If you don't, I'm leaving'. And I was not in control of events. I had got to the point where I had shot the hostage, actually. So I handled it badly and I basically said, 'I'm going'. Now, I was under pressure, but I couldn't control events. Other people were controlling events, not me. The timetable, what happened next – I was entirely reactive, I wasn't in charge of the agenda, I wasn't even contributing to the agenda. Those were three of the unhappiest months of my life. The level of pressure was no different, it really wasn't. The fact was, I had no control over it, and I know I was under stress. Pat and I don't row, but I was certainly horrible to be with during that time. I drank too much. I ate too much. I didn't exercise enough. I had all the classic symptoms of being under stress. I don't smoke, but if I did I would probably have been on 80 a day. I don't do drugs, but if I did I was probably going to be mainlining or something! For me this was a bad time, although others may have thought that there was nothing much wrong. It was only for about three months, but it was hard. There was one Sunday morning, a glorious autumn day, I was down at the bottom of the garden on the bench reading The Sunday Times and Pat came along with a mug of coffee, and she tripped and dropped the coffee on my paper. I went absolutely wild! And she stood there and said 'What on earth …? The newsagent is 300 yards away and it's only £1.25!' And I remember looking up at her and saying, 'What's happening to me?' And it was because I was not in charge of events.

So, the next day I walked into the office and said, 'That's it, I'm going'. I told the partners privately that I was leaving and we planned a way of working me out of the firm. I was back in control. Life was very difficult then with lots of pressure, but so what! It was *pressure*, it wasn't *stress*. There was a difference, I could see it, and I have never forgotten.

That's very interesting, I've never looked at stress and pressure in those terms before. When I feel stressed I tend to take it out on my kids.

And that it is because you have shifted from being in charge. You can be under enormous pressure, but if you are in charge of your own involvement in it to the point where you might want to say, 'I'm going', then you are in charge of it. When you lose control of your space, and somebody is running you, and you are reacting, you will do negative things: you will eat too much, drink too much, take it out on the kids, take it out on the missus – you will do something negative or destructive, because you are no longer in charge of events. In an information society it gets even worse because you walk in to the office and there are 47 emails, all with 'cc Digby Jones'.

Absolutely. So the picture I am getting is that you are blessed in many ways because you have a very good memory, you are good at prioritizing and you are good at delegating – and these are all pretty essential skills.

And I monitor it myself.

Talk me through that.

I have a little expression which I often say to myself, and
certainly I say it to my PAs Matt and Aimée sometimes and my
wife Pat at other times: I say it's 'not my finest moment', which
means that I know I could have done better. I have no problem
in knowing when I was very good and I also know when I could
have done it better. I sit and analyse how I could have done it
better.

So you learn for next time?

Yes you do. I do that. I sit down and I think, now where and how
could that have been better? And sometimes nothing you did
could have made it better, but sometimes it could. And
sometimes it's that you've got away with it. I know I have
sometimes winged it, I have come away and thought 'Thank God
for that', when actually I wasn't fully equipped with the
information and everything else, but I got away with it. But
always be honest with yourself.

One of the other things I do is, I always read my brief.
Always. Because in my job I used to see politicians who hadn't
read their brief, and it was pathetic to see. So I've always read
my brief. Even if it means I'm ten minutes late because I'm sitting
in the car reading it before I walk in, I always do it. Fortunately,
because you are often travelling you can read your brief on the
hoof. But read the information, analyse it, be prepared.

Communication

I found Sir Digby Jones's distinction between pressure and stress both fascinating and, from a personal perspective, very useful. However, I wanted to look in more detail at the principles of 'priority' and 'memory'. I have no doubt that both are vital in the effort to manage information. However, I have known a few corporate lawyers in my time, and I have witnessed the reading and assimilation that they have to do to prepare for a case – the paperwork alone is often measured by the box. I wondered whether the corporate lawyer relies on other tools and techniques to stay on top? Having been a corporate lawyer himself for almost a decade, I wondered how Sir Digby had coped.

I'd like to ask about your time at the law firm Edge & Ellison. I once worked for a company which bought another company, and the paperwork involved was immense. There were three directors in this publishing company, and we all spent many weeks reading the papers. I didn't feel that I had any control over it at all. Then a corporate lawyer came in to advise us, went through the paperwork in probably about 25 minutes, and already knew more about what was going on than I did. Is that just memory? What skills are involved there? You must have been involved with these sorts of things time and time again?

Oh yes. The one thing that corporate lawyer had wasn't the knowledge he possessed of the deal, it was his ability to communicate it to you. He obviously had the ability to distil the knowledge, handle it, and then communicate it to you because the one thing we haven't talked about, and perhaps we should now, is this ability. You can have all the information in the world, you can prioritize yourself, but if you can't communicate it you are dead. And he obviously had the ability to take all this information and say, 'Let me simplify it for you'. He wouldn't be patronizing you, but he would simplify it for you, and he would make it easy to understand.

He was talking my language?

Yes. That's what a good lawyer does. It is a skill. Can you learn it? Yes, you can become a better communicator. Are you born that way? Yes you probably are actually. My old Housemaster at Bromsgrove (who sadly died in September) always used to tell this story, whenever I went back for Old Boy Days. He taught Biology and he said, 'I can remember one day explaining something in Biology at O level, and this guy at the front of the class was sitting there, and he was finding it very, very difficult, and I looked up, and you were at the back of the class talking to your mate and looking out of the window. And when I'd finished explaining it I said, "Right Jones, maybe you might like to talk us through it".' Then he said, 'What really pissed me off was that you came to the front of the class, and you did it! And what was worse, the bloke at the front said after that, "Oh I understand it now sir!"'

That's a lovely story. But I bet the chap you were chatting to at the back didn't get it!

No, he wouldn't have got it – he probably failed his Biology O level. And it's the ability to explain it in words that people understand, because you get no prizes for showing somebody you are really clever if they haven't understood it. It is very important.

So maybe it's not just assimilating the knowledge, but it is also being able to communicate it – interpret it and then communicate it?

Yes, and it's also important to look at how you handle the information. I mean it's that old cliché, isn't it – 'I'm sorry this letter's so long, I didn't have time to write a short one'.

I'm a copywriter, so I face that all the time!

It's your job, isn't it, to distil it down. I did an article before I went on holiday and they wanted 400 words on a particular subject, and I wrote down all my thoughts, and when I counted it up it was 1,800 words, and the skill was to get that to 400 without losing the flavour of the article. That took an ocean of time. Writing down 1,800 words, just dumping my thoughts, that was straightforward. I'd like to think they were rather good thoughts, but it was not the most difficult thing in the world to do. The difficult thing was to hone it to 400. Now that is the ability to communicate efficiently and it is very, very important.

People are kind enough to say things to me like, 'You were on Radio 4 and in one minute I understood the issue'. I didn't have any training for it. I arrived at the CBI and they said, 'Right, we are going to send you on media training', and I said, 'What for?' And they said, 'Well you've never had any'. I said, 'I have been recruited to be me, and I'm a quick learner, I'll make loads of mistakes, but I am going to be me'.

That is very interesting. When I was talking to Andy Green, he said that he had had all sorts of problems when he first stood up to talk or present, until his trainer said that he should just stand up and be himself. After that, he said, he found it very much easier.

Yes – I mean, if you stand up and be you, what you've then got to learn to do is to fine-tune yourself, but you haven't got to try to be someone else, and there's a big difference. You know, people say to me, 'We've asked you for a 30-minute speech, not a 40-minute speech'. Now all I've got to do is distil me, or to get my feelings into a one-minute interview with John Humphrys. I am still me, I've just got to look after me, whereas if somebody says, 'Right, well you are not going to be you, you are going to be a different sort of person', then you'll get found out. They'll have you – interviewers such as Jeremy Paxman or John Humphrys will eat you for breakfast!

Well I was going to say that there must be times when you're glad that you've got some self-confidence ...

Well, that grows over time.

The long hours culture

Although I felt armed with some very practical techniques for managing information personally, I still felt that organizations have been slow to react to the amount of information that their employees are obliged to manage. There is a need for organizations to create a culture where knowledge is shared between people and teams on a systematic basis. I wondered if the long hours culture was another by-product of the information age, and whether Sir Digby Jones was a supporter of it.

I've worked in so many organizations where the culture is, that if you are not in at eight in the morning, and if you are leaving the office before half past seven at night, then you are obviously not doing your job properly. Is the long hours culture something that irritates you?

Actually no. I'm a long hours guy. I am trying to be very honest with myself here. When I was at Edge & Ellison and I was clambering up the greasy pole I would get in for about half-seven in the morning, and if we weren't going out to a dinner or something I would leave at about half-seven at night. As I started to build a team, and be in charge of a team, I don't think I ever said to somebody, 'I'm expecting you to stay late', but they did anyway.

Why?

Because the boss did. And I would be lying to you if I said I hadn't. It would be the easiest thing in the world now to say to you, well you know they are barmy if they work long hours. What I did do though, to be fair, is I'd say to somebody, 'Nothing you are doing now cannot wait until tomorrow, so you are not impressing me by doing it now. Go home'. Or, 'You've got your kids' sports day or something, go and do it'. But if it had to be done for tomorrow, oh yes, I expected them to work through the night, and I really did expect it. And at the CBI I used to call my first meeting 'morning prayers' and I used to have all my close people together at nine o'clock Monday morning but always held my first meeting in the office an hour before that.

OK, setting the tone for the week ...

Yes, so my wife and I used to leave our house in Warwick on a Sunday night at about ten o'clock, get to London at about half-eleven, go to bed, get up refreshed and ready to call my first meeting at eight o'clock Monday morning, so you start bang, eight o'clock Monday morning. I make no apology for that because, as I said earlier on, there is no substitute for hard work. That does mean you put the hours in. But you see, working harder doesn't mean working more hours, it means applying yourself, possibly exhausting yourself, but doing it within that time-frame. It was half-seven when Matt and I left here the other night because something had to be done for the next day, and frankly, I have no idea what time he is going tonight but if he's not out of here at five I'll be amazed. It is not my problem ... just get the work done.

So it's in line with necessity?

Absolutely, it's in line with necessity. The long hours culture is where people stay because it is the ethos of the place to work long hours. It ought to be a results-based culture. Now in a results-based culture you probably have to work long hours, but not all the time, and you probably have to work hard, but you are driven by performance. I give A for achievement, not E for effort, that's a given.

OK, what I am hearing, though, is that whatever time of night it is, you get home, you shut your door and that is the end …

Yes, that is the end.

Until the next day, or the next week, or until you're back from holiday, or whenever it might be?

Yes. When I was in corporate law I used to do the through-the-night big completion meetings; I knew one completion meeting that went on for three days – you would be in over the weekend doing it. When I was at the CBI I would do a speech after dinner most nights or I'd be travelling most nights. I work the evenings in the week, and people always used to say to me, 'God, you work hard', and I used to say, 'Nowhere near as hard as I used to work at Edge & Ellison!' I would get into bed about 11-ish, and the alarm would go at half-five in the morning. I've only ever needed between five-and-a-half and six hours' sleep a night, all my life – I can't remember the last time I had seven hours' sleep. Even as a kid, my mum says I never stayed asleep for long. And I sleep like the dead! When I checked out of a hotel the other week they said, 'Sorry about the fire alarm last night', and I said 'What fire alarm?' I hadn't even heard it! I sleep really well. I have never taken anything to help me sleep, I have never taken a pill in my life. I sleep on planes. I slept when my first wife left me! I sleep when I've got a big, big deal the next day. Even when I've messed something up and I'm going to get a bollocking the next day, I still sleep!

That sounds like a pretty essential skill.

Yes, I think it is. Harold Wilson once said, didn't he, that he always slept well. And Margaret Thatcher has said that she always sleeps well.

Have you always set goals? Have you always had an end in mind, or a target in mind? Clearly when you were 20 you didn't think, 'In 15 years I am going to be Director-General of the CBI' I'm sure, but did you think, 'I'm going to be a hot-shot corporate lawyer'?

Yes.

At what stage did you know that?

When I joined Edge & Ellison I was 23 and an articled clerk, now called a trainee, and my ambition was to be senior partner. I was going to be senior partner, and I wanted to be the youngest senior partner, and I did it. But when I was Director-General of the CBI my ambition was to change the organization and make a difference. I couldn't become Senior Director-General!

But there was an achievement in mind?

Oh yes, it was to increase the membership, to increase the public profile and to get the spirit going internally.

One of the things I expect that I will find quite challenging now is that, for the first time since I was 25, I am performing a role in which I have no executive responsibilities at all! I am an advisor. I am going to find this very strange but it is just one more challenge to meet and overcome.

I am sure that I not alone when I say that I have worked for companies where employees hoard knowledge, regarding it as a way to protect their position. What can an organization do about that? Worse still is when those same employees then resign, taking that knowledge with them to a rival organization. Again, what can be done? I remember in my first job as a shop assistant in Stanfords, the map and travel bookshop in Covent Garden in London, there were three employees who survived in that store for ten years only because they knew so much about the stock they sold. They wouldn't have survived in any other business. Yet no one dared to get rid of them.

Quite. I remember at Edge & Ellison we had one partner – a brilliant lawyer – and he would say, 'Only I can do this'. Why? 'Well I'm the only one who knows it.' Well why don't you share that with someone else and they could do it? 'Oh no, no, no, no, no.' And you could just see that what he'd got stamped on his forehead was *insecure*.

So in your CBI days, what would you have advised particularly smaller organizations to do?

I used to say, you have got to move out of commodities, those goods and services that sell only on price. You have got to get into knowledge-based innovation. You must invest in kit and in people.

Kit as in IT?

IT – yes. And then what you must do is sell that knowledge to the world at value added prices.

OK, and what should they do internally?

Internally it's unrelenting isn't it? It comes from the top of the business. I've always maintained that people work for you and in your business through 'QED'. And it's in that order: The Q is the *quality* of what you do. The quality of the work that people are provided to do. The quality that is the reputational issue of the business.

The E is the *environment* in which you work. Is it a friendly place to be? Do people have a laugh? That comes from the top. I've always thought a little bit of teasing, nicely done, obviously not bullying (if you see a bully, sack him!), but a bit of teasing, a bit of joshing – Monday morning, your football team, all that sort of stuff – is healthy. And when I read women writing this stuff about, 'Oh it's dreadful in our office, they all talk about football'. Well of course they talk about football – they are human beings! You know, if you met two women at the water-cooler you'd talk about whatever women want to talk about – it might be football or it might not! Nothing wrong with it! And if you get that spirit of the environment in which you work right, then you do begin to break down those barriers of me, me, I, I.

At the CBI I used to have my door open always, and I always used to make sure people understood when I had forgotten to do something. So I used to shout out to Matt who was outside something like, 'Oh God, I'm sorry, I forgot!' And I used to make sure people heard me say it, because if they hear you say it they might become brave enough to say it themselves. And then I used to say to someone down the corridor, 'Can you do me a big favour, I'm not good enough at this, I don't understand this, you do. Could you do it?' And I remember one day, Matt rang me when I was in the car and he said there are two ways to get you to your next appointment – one is to get back in the Daimler and be driven around, but actually if you walk up that alleyway and turn right up the steps you'll be there. I said, 'OK I'll walk'. And he said, and I heard him do it, he said – 'Everybody be quiet, the Director-General is walking. The Director-General is walking – stop the presses!' And I thought: I've won this because they were teasing me, they were doing it with quite a bit of affection in their voice, they were admitting that we had created a good environment.

Then the third thing is D, it's the *dosh*. The money has got to be right. You can persuade people to work for less but you can't persuade people to work for a lot less. They have to have the dosh – they have to be able to pay the mortgage, go home at nights. One of the universal standards of appreciation is money. I've never understood why somebody wants a million when they have already got a million. I've never understood that because I don't want to die wealthy, I want to die fulfilled and happy. But we live in a free society and I am delighted the world's best talent want to work and be paid here rather than anywhere else. If you don't pay people the going rate they will feel you don't appreciate them and vote with their feet.

A friend of mine who is a multi-millionaire – and I don't know whether it's his phrase or whether he read it in a book – he says, 'Don't pay the going rate, pay the staying rate'.

Very real.

Just picking up on the idea of sharing knowledge between workers at all levels in an organization, do you think that has almost created and caused the growth of CRM (customer relationship management) systems, for example?

Yes I do. There are two sorts of knowledge, aren't there? There's the keeping people constantly aware of their working environment, what's going on, using knowledge and information dissemination to get people to feel they belong and to get people just reacting as human beings. Then there's the second part of knowledge dissemination, which is what they need to do their job. There's the technical professional information they need, and in that the manager has to help the recipient of the knowledge by not just sending everything, but just sending what they need and probably sending a little bit more than they need, but not everything. You know, the easiest thing in the world is just to dump 40 pages, whereas actually they probably only needed a summary. But it is very important, and that's the manager's call.

And the cc on the email is another example?

It's a very good example. As I have climbed up the tree I find this often: managers taking responsibility for things they don't even know are happening, and nor *should* they know are happening. When journalists write, 'Why didn't so-and-so know what was going on?', well – get real! He's running 40,000 people and God knows how many offices – get real! Life's not like that. Take responsibility for it, definitely, that's why you're the boss, but to be expected to know it all – not a chance.

Very interesting indeed. Just talking about the fact that in the knowledge-economy, using your definition, we have got people who feel more confident – feel more empowered, frankly – to move to another organization that might be offering something more appealing. What measures can an organization put in place to try to prevent that happening?

Well there is a danger of course, because the one problem with moving to a knowledge-based economy is that when your assets go home at six o'clock at night, when they actually walk down the road to another job, they take all the knowledge with them as well, and it is pointless saying, 'Well I won't skill these people because when I've skilled them they will leave me'. You know, welcome to life.

So it is QED again?

It's QED. And by the way, some you are going to lose. You are going to train them and they are going to leave. But there are going to be others that someone else has trained that you're going to get. So the dynamic has changed about how you recruit, what you look for and how win or you lose. I saw this change at Edge & Ellison. I can remember when I was head of the department, if we lost one of our lawyers it was as if the world had ended. What had we done wrong? By the end of it when I was Senior Partner you'd be losing some every month and you'd be winning some every month. The world has changed in that respect.

So what can you do to keep them? QED. And you want them to take pride in what they do and where and how they do it. The other thing you do of course, is you have got to succeed as a business because people will stay with a successful business. The other important thing you have to do – and this is more relevant to customer bases – is to make sure they understand that if they walk out of the door they don't take the customer list with them, and if they do you will sue them.

So you need those measures in place.

You do, and you need your people to understand that you will do it. You know, if you are approached by someone else who says, 'Come and bring your client base, bring your information', well you can come and bring the stuff that's in your mind. But don't put the rest on a DVD and take it out of the building – if you do, we will sue you.

And there are enough protection measures and contracts and the like to make that possible?

Yes. That's the other point isn't it? You have got to set out the football pitch on which you're playing and where the goalposts are. You have got to say, 'There are some rules here'.

At the CBI I used to tell my people: 'If you come and tell me you have made a mistake, it is then my problem, not yours. You've done the thing you should do. You have admitted you've made a mistake. I am now there to help you and to help the organization sort it out. And you will usually find there is nothing new in this world and someone, somewhere in this organization will have made precisely that mistake in the past – there's a way of getting out of it 90 per cent of the time. But if you lie to me, I shall sack you because it is not fair on me, or the team that trusts each other. But if you are prepared to come and tell me you've made a mistake, fine, although I'd rather you hadn't made it, and if you are making too many of them we might have to have a conversation about life, but you will never get shouted at, you will never get bollocked, and you will certainly more than likely go up in my estimation.' I really used to say that – and it worked.

And people knew that you meant that.

People knew it! And they respond to it.

I am sure they do! And of course the last bit was the important bit. If somebody did actually lie to you and you said, 'Well, take it as a warning', then presumably you lose that sense of credibility?

I can remember somebody came to work for me on secondment from one of the big firms of accountants, and I said all that to her. On about the third day I said, 'By the way, where's that thing you were going to do for me?' And she said that she had done half of it. So I said, 'Great, can I see what you've done? Let me see how far you've got'. She replied, 'Well it's only in rough'. So I said, 'That's OK, I just want to see it'. Eventually I said, 'You haven't done it at all, have you?' And she said no. I said 'Good, because if you'd said yes you would be going back where you came from'.

I said, 'Well done, now I suggest you do it'. What was she going to try to do? She was going to try and tell me what she thought I wanted to hear, instead of telling me the truth.

You've just made me swallow because I've been guilty of that ...

Well we all have! I do it, we all do it, don't we? We are all human beings again. But this is something else in an information age that we have to be careful of. I don't know the answer to this, but people will tell you, write to you, send you, what they really legitimately, and honestly, sincerely believe is the truth. It happens to be erroneous. Something happened last week and I tell you, I would have gone in a witness box on oath and said X was X. Factually X was Y. I actually said to somebody, 'Oh it's so-and-so', and I really genuinely believed it, I wasn't lying. It happened not to be accurate. It was true as I saw it, but it wasn't accurate.

And that's an inevitable result of the age we live in?

It is, it's the age we live in. It's an inevitable result of it really, because everybody, from me to the taxi driver, is keeping more balls in the air than they have ever done before.

The impact of IT

I was aware that we had yet to discuss in detail the impact of IT on the information and knowledge economy. I knew that Sir Digby Jones was not a huge user of IT himself, but as Director-General of the CBI, he must have seen first-hand the impact and influence that it was having on industry and the workplace.

I asked him if he thought that we focus too much on the systems – the hardware and the software – to interpret information, rather than on the information itself. In the knowledge economy, is the reliance on IT essential?

It is essential, because that is your portal into being able to make the decisions, prioritize, discard, concentrate, focus. You have got to have those systems to download and dump information into you. You've got to. The problem is, where are your gatekeepers? What sort of world are you going to live in? Are you going to deal with all this? Is your PA? Are you going to have screening? What are you going to do?

It is interesting, isn't it, that the three things that are the real spur to consumerism's handling of information are football, pop music and porn, and those three things are really the mainstay of the consumerist IT revolution. Now what we've got to do is enable the profit to be made to invest the money to get even better, and at the same time ensure that society is protected a little bit from itself, and also ensure that we train people to handle the information and the knowledge. That's the answer. There is a little bit of 'ban it', but really you've got to train people to handle it.

Certainly the impression I get is that in earlier stages of the development of this knowledge economy we were very good as a nation at installing very sophisticated databases and other technology to store data without really giving any thought to what really needs to be retrieved and how to interpret what needs to be retrieved. Is that still true, or was that never true?

Oh yes, I think it is true. I'll give a very good example. My wife Pat's great-auntie died recently, and we are sorting out her estate. So we wrote to British Gas to say that Mrs Thompson has died, may we have a final account? And we get one, no problem, and they addressed it to the executors of 'Mrs Thompson deceased', fine, done. So can you explain to me why on Friday we got a letter from British Gas addressed to 'Mrs Thompson deceased', asking if she would like to buy winter cover against a faulty boiler?! And I really did do this – I rang up the number, pressed one, pressed three, pressed seven, waited an age and finally got through and I said, 'Somebody typed that in. I am not going to blame technology because a human being typed that into a database. A human being did it, and they must therefore have typed in the word "deceased". Has it crossed your mind that that means this woman is dead?' Now there's no excuse for that. That is a human being issue. I don't like it when I have to press one, press three, press seven, wait, get told 'Your call is important to us' but I'm still going to make you wait. I fully understand that if I don't want to pay huge bank charges every month, as someone with a pension fund that's got shares in banks, I understand why I need to make a profit and all of that, but when the human being element lets itself down, then we can't hide behind technology. The human element in a knowledge-based economy is enormously important and we're not very good at that. And in that we have become worse.

Yes, inevitably. You may have waited longer for a reply 15 years ago but when you got a reply, it would be personalized and it mattered.

Absolutely right.

The legacy

Finally, can I just read you a quote of yours, shortly before you left the CBI? You said:

> *'To whoever takes the job, I would say that they have to get out and about. I spend two days a week travelling, talking to people. Also you have to do the work. You have to read the briefs, otherwise you get caught out.'*

Is that the best tip to pass on to your successor?

The best tip is, if you are going to make a difference you have got to be able to lobby those who make the rules. By and large, these are politicians, and the route to public approval of what you are saying is the media. You are going to impress both the media and the politicians far more if you know what you're talking about. To be able to say to them, 'I was in Newcastle last week and I found that X, Y and Z', or 'I was in a school in Somerset and the Head Teacher said to me X, Y and Z' – then they listen, because it's real stuff. The greatest way of doing the job well is to get out and about. And sometimes, you don't want to. Waking up on a very wet, dull, grey Friday morning in Middlesbrough isn't really my idea of fun, but it arms you with the essential tool to do the job. And what is it? It's people.

True, you've got to be bright, and you've got to read the briefs. But if you go out and visit a business in Nottingham and then do an interview with the local newspaper, then people like Mervyn King or Gordon Brown will take more note of what you say. Ultimately, you'll have a greater effect on society and you will do your job better, and make more of a difference and isn't that why we're here? To maximize the talents we are lucky enough to have to make a difference for the better.

Conclusions and recommendations

I remember reading in a newspaper article that Deloitte were delighted to secure Sir Digby Jones's services, not because of his experience as Director-General of the CBI, but because 'he's a bloody good businessman'. He certainly comes across as someone that you'd like to do business with. I'm quite sure he would be a tough negotiator, but there would be nothing underhand in his actions. He is straight talking, honest and exceedingly good company.

He has certainly mastered the art of managing himself. He will work long hours when necessary, and has done throughout his career. But he will take every holiday day he is owed, and when he gets home, his working day is done. He would certainly acknowledge that he has the balance between his work and home life under control. He is blessed with a very good memory, and he is a fast reader, both of which help him to keep on top of his workload, and to manage the information that passes his desk. He delegates responsibly, and looks back and learns lessons from things he could have done better. He has learned from experience the importance of prioritizing his workload. Put these together, and the result is someone who seems always briefed, and always prepared. I was interested to learn that he would rather be ten minutes late, and prepared, than to arrive on time having not prepared properly.

In the twenty-first century, the biggest inhibitor of effectiveness and creativity in the workplace is stress. Sir Digby draws a key distinction between stress and pressure. We all face pressure, and must learn to accept it and deal with it. But stress is pressure over which we have no control, and that is the killer. We must get back the control in order for the stress to dissipate. His own experience of the effect that stress had on him certainly struck a chord with me.

It was refreshing to hear that protecting and sharing an organization's knowledge, and turning it into intellectual property, is no easy task. You can ring-fence and patent what you have as much as you like, but sometimes the best route for an organization is to accept that it can run with an idea for a good six months before it is stolen and copied. And those are the words of a corporate lawyer!

What of encouraging people to share the knowledge that they have, for the betterment of the organization as a whole? Again, Sir Digby argues, this is harder than it sounds. People who retain knowledge, and refuse to share it, are often insecure. The answer is to create a 'QED' culture: People feel secure and empowered by the *Quality* of the work that they do, and the *quality* of the organization's culture. They are driven by the *Environment* in which they work, and also by the *Dosh* that you offer them. If you can provide QED, and your staff still won't share their knowledge within the organization, then it's time for them to go.

It is very hard not to like Sir Digby Jones. He is interesting to listen to, and seems genuinely interested in what you have to say. He is straight talking, and his advice is highly practical and down to earth. He doesn't have all the answers, and he is perfectly prepared to say so. When I thanked him for sparing the time to talk to me, he said that he had thoroughly enjoyed every minute. What was so refreshing, was that he clearly meant it. And do you know what? I enjoyed every minute too.

Managing information and knowledge checklist

If you are looking for ways to manage the information and knowledge in your organization, here are some issues to think about. You might want to find a few, valuable minutes to take a clean sheet of paper and jot down any ideas that the following list generates.

The impact of knowledge

'Without it, we are dead' (Sir Digby Jones). So what are you doing about it? How do you sift through information to identify what is important and what's not? How do you prioritize, and how could you prioritize more effectively? What measures could you introduce to educate your people how to handle information better? Could you delegate more? Could you delegate more effectively?

Habits

Do you copy people into emails unnecessarily? Why do you do it? Is it absolutely necessary? Are there procedures in your organization that create red tape? Are they necessary? How could you simplify them? Could you get rid of them altogether?

Yourself

How effectively do you manage yourself? How good is your memory? Could you improve it? How? Do you find yourself 'winging it' when presenting or attending meetings? Would you be more effective if you were late, but prepared? Are you able to look back and admit that something 'was not your finest hour'? Do you analyse what you might have done better?

Stress and pressure

Do you agree that stress is pressure that is beyond your control? Are you under pressure or under stress? Looking at the stress in your role, what can you do right now to claw back control of the situation? Will you actually do it? Do you work long hours? If so, why do you? Does your organization have a 'long hours culture'? What has caused it? Do you take your full holiday entitlement? Do you work at weekends and in the evenings? How well do you sleep? What changes are you going to make?

Protecting and sharing knowledge

What can you do to protect the knowledge invested in your people, and turn it into intellectual property? Are there legal steps you could take to protect your intellectual property? Are they worth it? Are you better off accepting that your competitive advantage won't last indefinitely? Do your people share the knowledge that they have? If not, is it because of insecurity? What measures could you introduce to encourage sharing of knowledge? How does your organization rate in terms of 'QED' (quality, environment, dosh)? What role does IT play in storing data for creating shared knowledge?

Dianne Thompson on managing activities and resources

Dianne Thomson, Chief Executive of Camelot Group plc, operator of the UK National Lottery

'I think that we demonstrate a number of behaviours [at Camelot], including creativity and a partnering attitude, but another very important behaviour that we believe in is passion.'

Dianne Thompson joined Camelot in 1997 as Commercial Operations Director, although everyone remembers better when she took over as Chief Executive in 2000 after Camelot was awarded the second licence to run the National Lottery following lengthy legal proceedings. As Chief Executive, she has developed and driven Camelot's strategy for growth, which has succeeded in delivering the largest rise in National Lottery sales in eight years in the financial year 2005/06.

In a career spanning more than 30 years, she has held marketing roles for a variety of organizations such as ICI Paints, Sterling Roncraft and the Signet Group. She was Director of Marketing at Woolworths in the early 1990s.

She is a Fellow of the Royal Society of Arts, the Marketing Society, and the Chartered Institute of Marketing. She is also a Companion of the Chartered Management Institute and a liveryman of the Worshipful Company of Marketors. She has previously been awarded the titles of both Veuve Clicquot Business Woman of the Year in 2000 and Marketer of the Year by the Marketing Society in 2001. And she became the 'first lady of marketing' when she topped Marketing magazine's 'Power 100' list in June 2006. She also was named the Chartered Management Institute's Gold Medal recipient for 2006.

Dianne sits on the Press Complaints Commission, and is a member of the CBI President's Committee. In the 2006 New Year Honours list she received a CBE for services to business.

In today's high-pressured, time-poor environments, how can leaders and managers ensure that their staff are effective and motivated in their daily work? Is the drive for efficiency the responsibility of the individual or the organization as a whole? How does the culture of the organization affect its operational management? To have most impact, should a leader focus most attention on managing teams, or are energies better spent on optimizing financial resources?

These were just a few of the challenges that I wanted to discuss with Dianne Thompson, as I arrived at Camelot's London office in the Strand. Dianne was busy on the telephone as I took my seat, immediately reinforcing my assumption that she worked a relentless schedule. This seemed a good place to start to find out how Dianne regards all the various competing demands on her time.

Pressure and the work/life balance

Behind the principle of needing to manage activities and resources effectively, there is this assumption that today's workplace is 'high-pressured' and 'time-poor'.

High-pressured, time-poor – is that how you see your working life?

It is certainly how I see my working life, but I try very hard for that not to be the case for the rest of my people. I always describe Camelot as a way of life and not a job, but I do try very hard to make sure that the rest of the team get some sense of normality. To make sure that this is re-enforced throughout the company, we have a number of policies which have been devised to make sure that staff are protected and that they are able to maintain a healthy work/life balance while carrying out their often demanding jobs.

For example, we have comprehensive arrangements in place to allow flexible working practices like job sharing, phased return to work after prolonged leave, working from home and extended maternity benefits.

We do also have a comprehensive reward structure in place at Camelot to maintain the high performance culture that we have worked hard to put in place. We have annual progression pay reviews, an annual bonus scheme, an instant reward scheme based on a points system for staff who go that extra mile, as well as private health insurance, subsidised health club membership, company phones and cars, and a pension scheme where Camelot matches employee contributions by up to 7.5 per cent.

You said Camelot is a way of life, not just a job. What does that mean?

Well, we have daily draws now, we have three big draws a week – on a Wednesday, Friday and Saturday. So there are big retail peaks, and that makes us as close to being a retailer as you can get without actually being one. So when I get home at night, I look at the daily sales that have been sent to me. We are also more or less always a 24-hour business as people can play interactively now – through mobile phones, on interactive TV and on the internet – so even when the shops are closed the business doesn't stop. Senior managers within the business take turns at being the duty manager so there is someone on call

all the time – and I do my share of these stints, sometimes having to take calls through the night if big projects are happening and decisions need to be made there and then. So the job is there, all the time.

We are unique in that we are a private company but in a public goldfish bowl, and everything we do is under the utmost scrutiny, which is how it should be. But as the head of the company I need to be available nearly all the time.

So is there a 'typical working day' for you?

No, probably not, but I am not complaining. I absolutely love what I do. I try to have a bit of normality around the week. I try very hard to be in Watford (our head office) on Mondays and Fridays. I listen to feedback, and I'm often hearing people say that they 'like to see Di around'. So at least everybody in Watford knows that unless something unusual happens, I'll be there all day Monday and all day Friday. From Tuesday to Thursday, because of the nature of what we do, I tend to be in London, because that's where the media and the government are. In a typical week I try to limit the number of dinners I attend to two.

I try to protect Monday night. I live with my daughter, who has just started her first job here in London working for one of the big ad agencies. So we try to have Monday night as 'Mum and Jo night'. You do have to achieve the balance, because as I have said, Camelot is a way of life and not a job.

I have a quote here from Sir Martin Sorrell saying that women are much better than men at handling the work/life balance. I also have a quote from you saying: 'I'm just a workaholic. It is difficult to get

the balance right!' Is that still the case? Are you a workaholic?

I *am* a workaholic, but I think that is because of my background. I am the product of a Northern working-class family. My parents chose to have just one child to be able to give that child the opportunities they didn't have themselves. My dad, who is incredibly bright, had a place to go to grammar school but couldn't because his family needed him to go to work. It was a different generation. So they took the decision that they desperately wanted a family, but that they would only have one child so they could give that child the benefits that they hadn't had. And that child was me. So I think that they bred in me this sort of work ethic. That is where the drive came from, I think.

I became driven because I was trying to prove to them that their sacrifice was worthwhile. It is certainly where the inspiration came from. And, you know, people ask me if I have had mentors or role models. Well, my role models were my parents, because they tried so very hard. They brought me up to realize that you don't get anything for nothing, and that if you want something in life you have got to work for it.

I remember reading that while you were lecturing full-time at Manchester Polytechnic, you were also setting up and running your own advertising agency. Is that what you mean by working hard?

I like a challenge! The job at the Polytechnic was a sort of accident. I had worked for six years at ICI and it became clear to me that it was time for a change. I was invited to join ICI's fast track programme, which would have led me to a career in organics or petrochemicals. Flattered as I was, I knew that it wasn't for me. It made me think more carefully about my next step though and I realised that I wanted to 'give something back'. It might sound a little arrogant now – but that's what I wanted to do at the time.

Why do you think that was arrogant?

I think it was because I felt I had nothing to learn. The college persuaded me that they wanted people from industry to come in and give the students the benefit of some real experience. So I really did think I was going there to 'give', but that it would also be a very good time for me to think about what I wanted to do next. In reality, I learned so much and actually stayed there for seven years. Again, I was very lucky, because it gave me the opportunity to start my own advertising agency. It worked perfectly because the college was desperate to have people who were real, active practitioners, so they were keen to support me in starting the agency. And we were able to employ placement students in the agency while also getting agency clients to come into the college and do guest lectures as well.

People and the importance of culture

You only have to spend five minutes with Dianne Thompson to realize that she regards the people around her as her greatest resource. From the way I was welcomed at Camelot's reception desk, and then greeted by Dianne's colleague Charlotte, it was obvious that Camelot employees are a happy breed. I had read a number of articles and interviews with Dianne, where she had reinforced, time and again, just how vital the people at Camelot are to the company's success. I wanted to find out more.

One quotation stayed with me. About her staff, Dianne said, 'I know them and they know me'. Not unusual, one might think, until you realize that Camelot employs 960 people. I needed to find out the skills a manager needs to instil that degree of familiarity with almost 1,000 people.

How do you foster familiarity with a thousand people?

Well you see I am very lucky because we are a huge company. Our turnover last year was around £5 billion. But we employ fewer than 1,000 people. In fact, it is currently about 960. We are an SME (small and medium sized enterprise), and in an average year I get to see everybody at least twice. I try to get around all our sites. We have a warehouse in Northampton, sites in London and Aintree, regional offices whose main function is to pay prizes, and our biggest site at Watford, which is the head office.

As well as it being a conscious effort on my part to have that personal contact with as many of the staff as I can., there is also a lot of media interest in Camelot which allows the staff to find out more about me than they may do in less public facing companies. People will always stop me on the stairs and ask about how my daughter is getting on, how her degree was going, how her job is going – and this is from information they've read in interview that has appeared that week. And I think that's great – it creates a good working atmosphere.

So you don't mind that level of familiarity with your staff?

No, not at all. In fact I encourage it. We have worked very hard in the last six years to change the culture at Camelot after the company emerged battle-scarred and weary after the lottery licence bid in 2000. You may remember that we had a long, drawn-out legal battle before we finally won the second licence. And that had taken its toll on the staff. By May of 2001 we had lost one-third of the staff because while I had been out there fighting to try to save the business, everybody else was out there looking for another job. And who could blame them? We all have mortgages or rent and everything else to pay for.

By May of 2001 I had a company of 500 staff, trying to do the work of 800. And, all the time, we were trying to recruit and induct and train new people. So it was vital that we initiated a massive culture change to re-vitalise the company and to drive it forward. We really needed to change the culture almost overnight if we were going to succeed.

We started by taking the senior managers, of which at that time there were probably about 80, away in groups of about twenty on a three-day cultural programme called 'Winning Ways' We all had some ideas of the values in the company, and we went away to question whether these values were still valid in the new world we are in. If they were valid, how do we make sure that we get them embedded in the company, and do we need to have a set of behaviours that actually typify what we expect the values to be?

We had the mnemonic 'FITTER'. It stands for:

We believe in Fair play
We believe in total Integrity (We are totally honest, totally transparent. We have to be that way, because if ever you had any doubt about the integrity of the Lottery, then the Lottery is dead.)

We believe in **T**eam work

We are **T**rusted to deliver

We strive for **E**xcellence

We are **R**esponsible to all our stakeholders (Camelot is unusual because we have a massive number of stakeholders; from 30 to 40 million players a week, to retailers operating over 26,000 lottery terminals, to government, our regulator, 14 lottery distributors, public interest groups and NGOs – the list goes on.)

So those were our values beforehand. Then we went away and asked ourselves whether they were still valid for us today. And we agreed that, yes, they were. So how do we embed them in the company and what behaviour do we want to see?

I think that we demonstrate a number of behaviours, including creativity and a partnering attitude, but another very important behaviour that we believe in is *passion*. I know that you could talk to virtually anybody who works for Camelot, and they would agree. We are just passionate about what we do. We get up each morning to go to work to make Britain a better place. That's what we do!

But you are clearly proud of it?

I'm desperately proud of it. Camelot has helped to raise over £19 billion for good causes, which has helped to fund over 250,000 individual awards up and down the UK. That's in addition to what's gone into the Treasury in Lottery Duty. It has transformed the face of Britain and has paid for the biggest period of civic regeneration since Victorian times. How amazing is that?! Plus, we've now created more than 2,000 lottery millionaires!

I'd really like to investigate this culture a little more deeply. I can see how at head office in Watford, you could look around you, and you'd notice straight away if someone wasn't displaying one of those values, particularly the passion value. But you've got almost 1,000 staff. How can you be so confident that you all share the same values? How would you know if someone wasn't demonstrating the Camelot culture? What are the processes or mechanisms that are in place?

We moved from an annual appraisal system, which most companies have, to what we call 'quarterly goal-setting'. Take my colleague Charlotte as an example. At the end of each quarter, Charlotte will have a mini-appraisal with her line manager, who will review what she has done over the last three months against the objectives she was set. And she will be given a score which, at the end of the year, accounts for what we call 'progression pay'. At Camelot, if you have an exceptional year, you will get a progression pay bonus. But in that goal-setting meeting, Charlotte will also discuss what the goals and targets are for the next quarter, what development needs she might have, things that she is interested in doing that might expand her skill set, and the values and the behaviour that are part of that process.

Everybody is targeted with living the Camelot values and those values are instilled in the company all the way through. I am very privileged because I run a big company, we do a huge amount for good causes for Britain, and yet we are only 1,000 people, so we know each other. If you are in ICI with 200,000 people, how do you do that?

But there are companies with 40 people who don't have that, who are thinking 'how on earth do you do it with 1,000'?

The answer is, you need to be open and transparent.

It's as simple as that?

It's as simple as that. You are open and transparent, you communicate well, and you are passionate about what you do. It is a standing joke, but you can slice any one of us inside and we are like a stick of rock that says 'Camelot' or 'National Lottery' all the way through.

We are all working towards the same end.

And that's clearly something that exists informally in Camelot as well as formally? You have teams, and there are team structures, but it seems as though this team spirit comes pretty naturally?

Yes, I think it does. I think we learnt the hard way during our bid for the licence in 2000.

During a judicial review which became part of that competition, Camelot had such a high profile that the media were reporting on events incredibly quickly and before we had even had a chance to talk to the staff ourselves. So they were finding out what was going on from the television – which is not how I believe it should be!

It was a defining moment for me to understand that you can't always control your messages or the timing of when information is released. I realised then that we had to revise our mechanisms for talking to our staff quickly.

So we created our 'cascade process', and every Monday the executive team at Camelot has a meeting at ten o'clock, which lasts about an hour when we review what has happened over the last week, any issues we have, and what is going to happen that coming week. We decide on anything that the staff collectively need to know. We agree on the five or six points that should be cascaded throughout the company and then each of us cascades these key points to six or seven people. They, in turn, have a team of people to cascade to, and by 12 o'clock everybody in the company has received the key points of that week's meeting.

It keeps everybody informed, involved and very much part of the business – rather than perhaps feeling isolated in their own particular area.

What's the opposite of cascade? How would I, as a junior member of staff at Camelot, get a message back up to you?

Quite easily actually, because everybody knows that they are more than welcome to email me, or come and see me, or ring me. I have an open door policy. In a typical week, I would say that I probably get 20 or 30 emails from staff, with questions or suggestions for improvement.

But on a more formal level we also have a 'Staff Consultative Forum', which is a group elected to represent all of the departments in the company. The elections are supervised by ACAS, so it is all externally monitored and verified. The forum meets every six weeks as a body, and once a quarter they meet formally with me and the HR Director, so I am there by their invitation. That is their opportunity to share ideas with me, and I share my ideas with them.

This week, for example, they wanted to know how the current licence bid was going. The deadline for submission has just been extended, and they wanted to know what that meant for Camelot. They can also give me feedback on decisions we have made for the business, make suggestions for the whole business, or for their individual departments, make a complaint about something they, or members of their department are not happy with – and I take that information back to the executive team for consideration and action where necessary.

We also have a annual staff survey, operated and verified by an external company and the regular quarterly meetings each employee has with their line manager is another opportunity for individuals to formally feedback information they want to be cascaded upwards.

I'm intrigued by your cascading processes. I know of organizations where team leaders and managers 'filter' the information that goes back to the people at the top. In other words, they tell you what they think you want to hear. Does that exist at all here? Would you know if it did?

We don't do that at all. I think the issue is to do with integrity, as I was saying earlier. We are very fortunate that through good marketing we are here 12 years on, with 70 per cent of the adult population still playing the National Lottery. And that's because they believe it is totally fair and is run with complete integrity. The day that they don't believe that is the day that the Lottery will come to an end.

So we have to be absolutely transparent about everything that we do, and that's the way we run the business. Of course, we have to have some confidentiality regarding the bidding process, but in everything else, we are just open and honest.

So if a team leader has bad news, they will come and tell you?

Yes, absolutely.

And if you had bad news, you would tell the staff?

Yes, and we had an example last week. The bid schedule was put back by another two weeks.

How do I feel about that? I wasn't very happy. The reason I'm not happy is that there was a deadline that said 1 October, then it moved to 1 December, then it moved to 15 December, then the 26 January, and now it is 9 February. There are incredible pressures on the business to make sure that we get the best possible bid we can written and submitted, while maintaining business as usual and working flat out to make sure that we are fulfilling our role of making the best possible returns to Good Causes that we can.

Our business is running the National Lottery – and it's something I believe we do very well. Our business is not writing bids and all these false starts make it a lot harder on everyone.

Efficiency

'A good manager or leader increases operational efficiency and effectiveness'

Chartered Management Institute

I wanted to talk to Dianne about business efficiency, and what it means to an organization such as Camelot. In organizations of any size, whose responsibility it is to create efficiency? The individual employee, or the organization as a whole? I was fortunate enough to have read before the interview that Camelot runs the most efficient lottery in Europe. I asked Dianne how lottery efficiency was measured.

It is measured by the returns to government and good causes. There's an American company called La Fleur, which analyses and reports on lotteries worldwide. They investigate how much money goes back in prizes and also how much goes to governments and good causes. Some lotteries around the world don't differentiate between government and good causes – they simply make returns to government, and then government decides on the allocation. We pay lottery duty as well as give money to good causes. So it is that percentage of the total take that goes to government which is regarded as the measure of efficiency.

Did you set out to be the most efficient lottery in Europe? Was that one of Camelot's aims from the start?

We set out to be very efficient, simply because of how the lottery pound breaks down. On average, 50 per cent of the revenue generated goes back to players in prizes; 28 per cent goes to the good causes; 12 per cent goes in lottery duty, which is obviously a statutory duty – it's not optional. So that's 90 per cent of the revenue taken care of already! Then 5 per cent goes to the retailers – they get a 5 per cent commission on every ticket that they sell. They also get a small commission for paying the low-tier prizes.

So when all of that is taken into account, I'm left with 4.8 per cent of the revenue that actually comes into Camelot. Of that 4.8 per cent I lose one percentage point immediately: because we've got lottery duty on tickets rather than VAT, I can't reclaim the VAT that we spend in the business – so my 4.8 per cent becomes 3.8 per cent. Then after all of Camelot's running costs are paid for, we are actually allowed to make half a percent profit. So it's absolutely vital that I keep the costs tightly under control – if I let them drift by only half a percent, then my shareholders wouldn't get any return at all.

No wonder you take efficiency seriously. So it is as tight as that?

It is. We are different from a lot of other lotteries. For example, many state lotteries work very differently. A typical example would be one of the European lottery's which gives back 50 per cent in prizes to the players. They will give 5 per cent, as we do, to their retailers. So that is 55 per cent allocated, and 45 per cent remains. Then they will take their costs out of that 45 per cent and whatever is left goes into government.

Because it is measured in this way, there is no real incentive for them to be very efficient at all.

In contrast, this is the only job I have ever had where I am praised for making half a percent profit – everywhere else I would have been fired!

This was extremely interesting. I realized that I had never paused to consider how the National Lottery revenue was allocated – or even the fact that Camelot does not distribute the money, but merely collects it from selling lottery tickets and then passes it straight on to the lottery distributors who then decide how it is given out. Nor how it might vary so much between lotteries around the world. Maintaining Camelot's efficiency is clearly of vital importance to Dianne Thompson. But although Dianne describes Camelot as a small organization, it still employs almost 1,000 staff. How would she know if this is an efficient head count? Why not 900? What measures are in place to identify efficiencies throughout Camelot? I asked Dianne to tell me more.

We are constantly undertaking business reviews. We have a financial review group, which I chair, and we meet quarterly. But of course we have period reporting, so I am monitoring costs on a period-by-period basis. In terms of how we decide the optimum organization, we were 800-strong in 2000, and crept up to about 900 by 2002. We conducted a massive review of the organization at that time, which concluded that we needed to streamline things slightly, so we reduced the organization structure by about 80 people. Today, we are up to 960, but that's because we have gone into new areas. We now have a substantial interactive team because we sell on mobile phones, the internet and interactive television. We have also created our own design studio in-house. We looked at what we were spending with external agencies on design, and decided that we could do it far more cost-effectively if we built our own studio and recruited our own people.

So everything is constantly under review because, to be honest, if you are running a business on 4.8 per cent, which includes your profit, there's not much room for manoeuvre.

So would you advise any organization to undertake the sort of efficiency reviews that Camelot does? Is the drive for efficiency as relevant to other organizations?

Well businesses usually try to be efficient because they all have shareholders. Although we are not a publicly listed company, we have a commitment, a fiduciary duty, to make profits for our shareholders. So of course there's always this pressure on us to keep our costs down and to find new ways of being more efficient.

Let me give you a very specific example of something that we have done. We had three separate call centres at one stage. We had a telesales call centre, then we had 'hotlines' as they were called, a retailer hotline and a lottery hotline, each with their own trained staff. What we have done now is to multi-skill everybody, so anybody who operates in our call centre can now do each of those three things. That in itself has allowed us to become more efficient in how many people we need answering the calls.

So where should a business start when looking to make efficiency gains?

I think all I would say is that you need to be proactive all the time. I get very frustrated with the 'if it ain't broke, don't fix it' mentality. That's not the way to run a business. The way to run a business is always to be proactive: look for efficiencies, look for ways to drive sales, to drive profits. So many people in business leave it too late, until they get into trouble. We have an annual operating plan, and we conduct quarterly reviews, so that we could see quite easily and early if we were going adrift anywhere.

Project schedules and delivery

'A good manager or leader delivers on time, to budget and to the standard required'

Chartered Management Institute

Throughout my own career, I have worked with organizations for whom a key measure of success is the extent to which projects are delivered on time and within budget. From a personal perspective, I have lost count of the number of times I have worked late into the night, finishing a proposal or a report that had to be submitted the next day. Yet here I am interviewing the Chief Executive of Camelot, whose responsibilities include putting together a bid to run the National Lottery. I remember watching on television the sealed bids to run the National Lottery being delivered to the Department of Culture, Media and the Arts back in 1994. Pallets containing boxes of paperwork were being unloaded hurriedly from lorries in an attempt to meet the midday deadline. Just what skills or efforts are required to keep a project like a lottery bid on track? What measures does Dianne

Thompson have in place to ensure that the next lottery bid is delivered on time and to budget?

Right, well that's easier to answer than you might expect. I think one of the things that makes Camelot quite different from a lot of organizations is that we never get into 'steady states'. We go from one major project to another. Let me give you an example. When we won the bid last time, one of the conditions of winning was that we had to install brand new terminals in every retail outlet. There was a time-frame with a financial penalty if we weren't ready on time. The penalty was £1 million a day to start with. So that focuses the mind a little bit!

So that was a massive project to get the terminals installed, and in fact we got them all in two weeks early, which was great. Then the next big challenge was to transfer all of our software systems over, which was a massive undertaking. It's similar to the process that the passport control service went through, when they got into so much trouble. So that was our next big project.

Then one of our main software suppliers got into financial difficulties in the United States and went into Chapter 11 administration. So we decided to build an ISDN network, so that we wouldn't be dependent on them. Now we own the largest private ISDN network in Europe.

Life is never straightforward at Camelot; you are literally going from one big project to the next. That's what I mean when I say that there are no 'steady states'. Everybody is working on a project at all times really.

So how would I know that the bid is on track and on budget? Well for such a big project I have a bid director, who takes responsibility for the most complicated, critical tasks.

Each section of the bid has its own timeline, with a cost attributable to it for the research that might be needed to be done. There is also a separate production budget. We monitor the bid's progress at a bid steering group every week and I can see whether we are on track.

But if the pattern at Camelot is a constant flow of challenging projects, with little respite, what sort of toll does that take on you personally?

Well I am on record as saying this isn't a job, it's a way of life, and it is! It is very intrusive and very time-consuming, but I think in many ways that's part of the challenge and also part of the huge enjoyment, because you have a whole variety of different things going on all the time. It is very stimulating.

Monitoring finance

'A good manager or leader optimises use of financial and other resources'

Chartered Management Institute

Dianne Thompson's career history comprises a number of senior marketing roles, in some of the UK's best known corporations. She has 20 years of experience working with seven-figure marketing budgets at Woolworths, ICI and Camelot. I wondered whether Dianne would have any financial advice that might apply to any organization. After all, most of us work with marketing budgets that are a fraction of that size. So what advice would

Dianne offer about marketing budgets and campaigns that might apply to smaller organizations?

Actually, I think it doesn't matter so much what the size of your budget is, because the crucial thing is the return on the investment that you are getting. At Camelot, what we have is a series of very sophisticated return-on-investment models. So everything that the marketing team does – be it a piece of television advertising or a direct mail shot or whatever – is assessed beforehand to predict what the likely return on investment will be. Then we evaluate it post-event. So over the period of 12 years that we have been running the business we have learnt very well what returns we can expect from our marketing spend.

So, for example, we know exactly what return we expect if we advertise the EuroMillions major draw that is on tonight. The EuroMillions jackpot tonight is running at about £64 million. We have been advertising very heavily during the week; I think we have done about 200 television rating points. We know exactly what sort of return we will get from that and, of course, we will evaluate it next week anyway.

But it is about making sure that you can evaluate what return you are getting so that you are using the budget that you have available in the most effective way possible.

It never occurred to me that an organization the size of Camelot would review every flyer, every advertisement, every mailing to that extent. Do you think other organizations are complacent in that regard?

I think marketing as an industry in general is complacent, to be honest. As you probably know, I was President of the Chartered Institute of Marketing, and during my time there one of our big concerns was that too many marketers are not accountable for the money that they are spending. That is one of the reasons why boards in general find the marketing budget the easiest bit to chop because it is very difficult for some marketers to be able to defend why they need that money. By having the tools that we've got here, these return-on-investment tools, it is very easy to make a case to my board if we feel we need to spend a bit more money to do something specific.

Just to put our budget in context, it is a large budget, of course and as you would expect for a company with a turnover of £5 billion. It equates to about one-and-a-half per cent of our total sales revenue, but it is being spread across lots of different products. That's why we have to evaluate everything we do so thoroughly, not least because we have four of the top ten consumer brands in the UK. So the dilemma here is, for example, whether we should be giving more support to scratch cards or Thunderball? Or is the marketing budget better invested in Lotto itself? That's why we need these tools so that we can see where we get the best returns for our pound.

I know of many organizations who have separated the sales and marketing functions, and aren't able to calculate the return on investment for each marketing activity. Is that a serious mistake?

I wouldn't say it is a serious mistake, but it just means that you haven't got the information you really need to make sure you are utilizing every pound of marketing spend to the very best you can.

At Camelot, we've been able to use external agencies to help us build econometric models. Take the EuroMillions Rollover today, we have got a very good idea as to whether we are likely to get better returns from television advertising or radio or printed media.

And are you saying that if an organization like Camelot can calculate its return on investment so effectively, then organizations of any size should be able to do the same?

Yes – they may not be able to use quite the same sophisticated tools that we have, but I do think that there is a responsibility for marketers, in particular, to do their very best to evaluate the returns that they are getting for their marketing monies.

Thinking about Camelot's television advertising for a minute, how quickly would you know whether a particular campaign is achieving what you want it to achieve?

You usually know very quickly. There are two types of basic advertising that we do here. There is what we call 'generic brand advertising' and then 'specific tactical advertising', which would be for something like a Rollover or a Superdraw. With the specific tactical advertising, you know almost immediately how effective it is as it is reflected in the ticket sales.

For example, by half past seven tonight (which is the 'draw break' when tickets are no longer available to purchase for that particular draw) I will know what the sales are. I will start getting text messages on my phone from 5 p.m. today telling me what the sales are at five o'clock, at six, at seven and then at draw-break. So you know already what the impact has been.

The generic brand advertising is a little harder, but the principles are largely the same. For example, the National Lottery launched with one game in 1994 and so advertising that one brand under the crossed fingers National Lottery logo was simple and effective. However, by 2002 the lottery had expanded massively and we needed to differentiate between the different games on offer. So we launched a series of advertisements with comedian Billy Connolly, to introduce the new name for the main lottery draw as 'Lotto'.

I don't know if you remember the ads, but in one of them he was standing on a beach in Scotland and he said something like, 'Those people that run the National Lottery have decided to change its name. And guess what they are going to call it? *Lotto* ...' and then he looked incredulous at what a daft name it was. It was an educational campaign – and although it did receive some criticism within the industry, it very effectively achieved its objective with the playing public. You talk now to anybody on the street and ask them the name of the game that you play on Wednesday and Saturday, they would all say 'Lotto'. Everybody has forgotten that it used to be called the National Lottery game. So even for a generic campaign like that we had a very specific objective that needed to be met.

So you asked me how quickly we could tell if it worked. Probably on that campaign, it was about three months when you could see in our tracking research that the name change had definitely worked.

Priorities and deadlines

'A good manager or leader plans and prioritises projects and activities'

Chartered Management Institute

One of the things that has intrigued me throughout all six interviews is how people like Dianne Thompson juggle competing demands on their time, and how they decide which is the priority or deadline that is most pressing. Most of us in our working lives have all or part of our agenda set for us. If you are self-employed, your priorities are set, at least in part, by your clients. If employed, then a line manager often dictates what you focus on during the working week. But what about when you are the Chief Executive of Camelot? When Dianne Thompson arrives at her desk, either in Watford or in London, how does she decide what she should devote her energies to? I needed to find out about her priorities, and what motivates her to get something done.

That's a very good question. As I said earlier, a typical week for me would be two days at head office in Watford. I try very hard to be here on Mondays and Fridays I like everybody here to know that they can get to see me any time, drop me an email or whatever. If I can be here more frequently then that's great, because this is head office, and this is where the bulk of my people are. But some of my job is about meeting with MPs and the media, and of course they are often based in London, so that will take me into town frequently.

I have a meeting that I chair, with my senior executives, at ten o'clock on Monday morning. For example, this coming Monday we will review what happened in the business this week. We will look at the sales for EuroMillions, we will talk about the issues that we've got coming up next week like the annual staff survey, we will be talking about the marketing activities we've planned, and those sorts of things. That will then get cascaded throughout the business, and that's how the working week starts.

On a personal level, my diary is booked up weeks and weeks in advance.

So no two weeks are the same – but there are elements that you will try to incorporate into every working week?

Yes, that's right. We have several committees, like any other organization would. So, as I mentioned earlier, we have a Staff Consultative Forum, which is made up of representatives voted for by their colleagues, who represent the various departments in the company. They meet every six weeks, and I meet with them once a quarter, so that's in my diary. I chair our Corporate Responsibility Board, which meets to ensure we are not only running a successful – but a responsible – National Lottery. This group meets quarterly, and that's always in my diary. Then at the moment we've got the Bid Steering Group which meets once a week. We have a People Steering Group, which comprises two of my fellow Directors and me. This meets to monitor staff roles in the business, and also to consider recommendations for promotion. You asked me earlier about how I knew that 960 was an efficient head count, and whether I could be sure I had the right number of people. Well this steering group meets quarterly, and keeps that under review all the time. I also have a Finance Review Group where we make sure that our costs are on track and so on. And then there are a whole variety of other things: for example, there's an Olympic Steering Group, because as you know we have been asked to raise money for the 2012 Olympics.

So by the time you have put all of those in the diary there is a bit of a structure to my working week. If you overlay that with things like the bid, and all the reading I'm doing for that right now, then that's what keeps the variety there.

I can appreciate the variety. But given that any one of your staff would completely understand if you told them that you had been too busy to read or do something, what motivates you to get something done or finished?

Because it is a matter of personal pride, isn't it? And I am sure that that is true for most people actually. As I have said before, at Camelot we are driven by the mission that we come to work to make Britain a better place by raising as much money as we can in a socially responsible way for the good causes. When I'm out and about travelling I like to go and see projects where Lottery money is being spent. Take something like the Eden Project – it's absolutely stunning what that has done, not only for the project itself, but for Cornwall. And in London, there's Tate Modern, Tate Britain, the National Portrait Gallery, the British Museum, the Millennium Bridge, in Cardiff the Millennium Stadium, in Glasgow the Science Centre and the Falkirk Wheel a little further up in Scotland, the Odyssey in Belfast … the list goes on. That is the pride that we all get out of what we do.

That's what we do, we raise money for those projects, and that's what makes us get up and come to work, and that's what makes sure we do a damn good job and makes sure that we all meet our deadlines!

That's fantastic, but are you ever able to switch off? I have read about sportsmen and sportswomen who mentally warm up before a performance, and then unwind after it. Is that something you are able to do? Can you unwind, mentally, from one committee meeting to another?

Sometimes yes. There are times when I'll be in the car when I am heading into London from Watford. That's my thinking time. But I am very keen on getting the work/life balance right for all my people. In fact, this weekend I've got a lot of reading to do and it's not very easy to fit that into the working week. But on a typical weekend I don't work. I switch off. I will watch the lottery ticket sales with great interest on Friday night and on Saturday for the Lotto draw. I'll get the result of how many winners we've got and that is part of my weekend. But I'm very lucky. I live in a nice place, I've got a lovely garden that I'm getting back into doing. I also enjoy walking – in fact I did a 10k sponsored walk last summer and managed to raise £16,000 for Breast Cancer after match funding from Camelot – and the Grand Union Canal runs through the village, so there are some great canal walks. I've got lots of friends and good pubs in the village and I shall be out and about socializing. So I am very fortunate that I have a full life outside work as well, and that's what allows you to switch off. It is not about sitting down and doing nothing, it's just about getting stimulation from doing other things, I think.

But I can't claim that it has always been this way. I was always the person who worked at weekends, and when I went away on holiday I was always phoning in and checking up on people and projects. I don't do that now. I have got a very good arrangement with my PA who knows that I'm taking a week's holiday in the first week in January with my daughter. She knows exactly where I am, where I will be staying and the deal is that if she needs me, or if anybody needs me, she will be the only person who knows where I am. We also have a prearranged time of day I'll put my phone on and pick up any messages. It's not too intrusive, but it also means that I am not unreachable if I am needed. I have become very disciplined in making sure that I get the breaks at weekends and on holiday and I try very hard to ensure that my staff do the same. It would have to be a dire emergency for me to get anybody disturbed while they were on holiday.

Conclusions and recommendations

Dianne Thompson is a remarkable woman. She says that she knows her staff, and they know her. And that is absolutely true. In fact, in so many ways, she is a departure from the traditional image of a grey-suited CEO. She made me feel as welcome when interviewing her as if I had dropped by to visit a friend for a coffee. And that's the remarkable thing. I love my friends dearly, but not many of them would be able to run a global organization with an annual turnover of £5 billion.

So what makes Dianne Thompson so successful? For one thing, her passion is infectious, and it is clearly what drives her. She absolutely adores what she does each day. When she says that she 'gets up each day to make Britain a better place', she means it. If you heard that from an American corporation, you would be tempted to rush to the lavatory. When Dianne Thompson says it, it seems like the most normal thing in the world. So could Dianne Thompson run the National Lottery effectively if she didn't believe wholeheartedly in what it sets out to do? I honestly don't believe that she could.

Second, she values the people around her above every other resource. It's fascinating to listen to Dianne talking, and to appreciate that she regards nearly 1,000 people as 'her family'. Many would argue that an organization with a £5 billion turnover, and nearly 1,000 staff, is a large, international organization. Not Dianne Thompson. To her, Camelot is firmly an SME. Therein lies her success with her people. Since she regards Camelot as a small organization, it is clearly easier for her to create and instil the culture that so evidently exists, and which works so effectively.

Dianne admits that the essence of the National Lottery rests in its integrity: 'The day people cease to believe that the lottery is totally fair and run with complete integrity, that is the day that the Lottery will come to an end.' It's quite obvious that this integrity suits Dianne Thompson very well. She attributes much of her success with people to her open, transparent approach, and recommends this approach to any manager or leader.

This openness extends to the way that Dianne Thompson presents herself. There is no pretence, no attempt to behave or act in any way that doesn't come completely naturally. She didn't voice it, but it's absolutely clear that she has earned the respect and support of her people by being herself at all times. So do her people know Dianne as well as they think they do? The answer, I can assure you, is yes. She is a living embodiment of the phrase 'what you see is what you get'. And that is a major, if not *the* major, reason for her success.

Managing activities and resources checklist

If you feel under pressure, with too little time to manage too many activities, here are some issues to think about. You might want to find a few, valuable minutes to take a clean sheet of paper and jot down any ideas that the following list generates.

Work/life balance

Is your work and your time outside work in balance? Do you work long hours because you have to, or because you feel out of control? What steps could you take right now to redress the balance? Can you protect an evening each week for yourself? What is the equivalent of the 'Mum and Jo night' for you?

Passion

Are you passionate about what you do? Do you believe wholeheartedly in your organization's products or services? If not, think about what is driving you to succeed throughout your working week. Give some thought to what you *are* passionate about. Is it time for a change?

Be yourself

Take a look in a mirror. Are you 'yourself' at work? Are you aware of consciously playing different roles to achieve certain outcomes? For example, do you find yourself enjoying playing the 'tough guy', even though it's not really you? Would your colleagues and staff say that they know you? How well? Are you open and transparent? What effect would it have if you made the decision to be yourself from now on?from now on?

People and culture

Do you cascade information quickly and effectively to your people? Are your people able to share their ideas and concerns with you? Are your people your greatest resource? Do you know your people, and do they know you? How would you describe the culture in your organization? Are you proud of it? Is your organization's culture holding you back, or driving you forward? What can you do about it? Are you and all your people working together towards a common goal?

Efficiency

What measures do you have in place to monitor the efficiency of your organization? Would you know if a particular team or department was less efficient than others? What incentive do you have for introducing more efficient measures? Do you have an 'if it ain't broke, don't fix it' mentality? How often do you review how efficient your organization is being?

Project schedules and delivery

As a manager or leader, do you demand that projects are delivered on time, to budget and to the standard required? Do you deliver that yourself? Do you plan the steps you or your people will take to deliver a project? How often do you review progress made on a project?

Finance

Can you currently measure the return on investment for every marketing pound that you or your organization spends? Do you review the effectiveness of every flyer, every mailing, or every marketing activity that you undertake? What steps would you need to take in order to be able to do so? What is stopping you taking them? On balance, are you using your marketing budget effectively?

Priorities and deadlines

Is your agenda set for you, or do you set it yourself? What motivates you to get something done? If it isn't a matter of personal pride, then should it be? Do you work in a high-pressured environment? If you do, should you be doing so? Can you influence the environment in which you manage or lead? Do you often feel 'time-poor'? What steps could you take to win back some valuable time? Are you able to switch off?

Andy Green on managing yourself

Andy Green, Chief Executive, BT Global

'What do I think are the biggest things that most correlate with people getting to the top? A will and a desire to get there.'

Andy Green is a chemical engineering graduate from Leeds University. He began his career at Shell and later joined Deloitte Haskins and Sells.

There followed a career at BT, which has spanned almost 21 years. He has been Chief Executive of BT Global Services since November 2001, providing networked IT services to multi-site organizations globally. With a workforce of almost 30,000 people worldwide, BT Global generated £8.6 billion of revenue in 2006. He is also responsible for BT's internal information systems strategy and operations. Before BT Global, Andy was Chief Executive of BT Openworld, the mass market Internet services company, which he set on a path towards profitability.

He has been a BT Group board member since 2001, and a member of BT's Executive Committee since March 1995. He is a board member of e-skills UK, and was appointed a Director on the NAVTEQ board in March 2006.

Of all the interviews I had prepared for, the subject of 'managing yourself' was easily the most personal. After all, it would be challenging to question someone about how people should manage themselves without getting to the heart of how the person I was interviewing manages himself. If I was to do this chapter justice, I thought, I would need to establish what this person is like at home as well as at work. What are they like with people? How do they handle stress? How do they set their own agenda? How accessible are they to their colleagues and staff? What are their own goals and aspirations?

I needn't have worried. Andy Green, Chief Executive of BT Global, had also found time to prepare for our meeting before I arrived. He had thought about how he manages himself and had broken down what he wanted to say into five key topics: managing your time; managing yourself mentally; managing yourself physically; managing your image; and managing your growth. I was reminded of the assertion that if you need something done urgently, you should ask someone who is already busy. That statement was written with Andy Green in mind.

Dynamism

While preparing for my meeting, one of the documents I read was a paper published by the Chartered Management Institute. It said:

> *'Organisations and individuals need to be more dynamic if they are to succeed in today's global and competitive economy, but the energy levels required to be dynamic are heavily dependent on motivation.'*

I chose to kick off the interview by asking Andy if he agreed with this statement.

I think it is an insightful statement if you mean 'dynamic' in the right way, and could be completely misleading otherwise. People say lots of things about what makes a good leader, and the biggest correlation is intelligence. But not everybody is intelligent, and some great leaders are not particularly bright. But they are all dynamic in the sense that they are questioning and challenging and they don't believe that the status quo will lead to success in the future.

If dynamic means the ability to recognize that you have to change and evolve, then I absolutely agree with that. I would say that regardless of the personal characteristics of leaders, I can't think of anybody whom I would class as a great leader who is not dynamic in that sense. But if it is suggesting that a leader has to be dynamic in the sense that they must be able to step on the stage and say 'rah-rah' to a sales force, I don't agree with that at all. I think there are many great leaders who have never done that.

So I would absolutely agree if we mean dynamic in this questioning sense, the search for a better way of doing things, an awareness of what is going on around you, a belief that the world is changing all the time and an acceptance that we have to change to be successful. In that sense I believe 100 per cent that dynamism lies behind all great leaders.

Given that definition, do you look around you at your peers and your colleagues and see a lack of dynamism, or plenty of dynamism?

I think that in any large organization you are going to see more dynamic people rise to the top, although you'll find variations in that. I think it is very difficult to get good business results in the medium term without a dynamic view. I think there are a lot of companies out there who are quite complacent, and I have consistently said over the last three years that this is the most dangerous time to be complacent. The technology wave that we all talked about in the late 1990s is happening just a few years later, and if people aren't changing the way they are thinking about the world and globalisation, if they are not thinking about how technology is changing their business models and how they need to change – they will get left behind. You can see in every sector, that some people are really getting to grips with what is possible and others are falling behind.

It is very easy when you start a new job to change things. I think one of the challenges as you go through more and more business cycles is to rethink. When we have meetings I try to do them in different places, because anything you can do to keep the world looking different seems to me quite important.

So do you despair when you read about chief executives at BA who still print out their emails and pass their replies to their PAs?

Well, that is a different question I think. I recently heard a very good speech from the Chief Executive of a significant national body who stood up and said 'I don't have a computer'. Nevertheless, he still talked about the way they'd used database technology and deployed it to win a major International coup for the UK.

Managing your time

So Andy Green was endorsing the need for people and organizations to be dynamic, in the sense that they must recognize the constant need to question, change and evolve. I remembered reading that Andy had a passion and understanding of technology, and was a great believer that it will change people's lives for the better. So I asked Andy about how he used technology as part of managing himself.

On a personal level, I am completely embedded in technology. I am an active 'per the second' individual, but for most people that is not necessary. It is not necessary, not even good management at times, although I think personal management of time is very important, and technology can support that.

You mentioned that you are completely embedded in technology. Talk me through it. If you are sent an email, does something flash in your pocket?

Yes, absolutely. Technology-wise I like three things: my mobile phone, because I am an avid texter and phoner; my Blackberry, which I carry around the world, rather than a laptop; and my iPod, which I carry around the world for all sorts of reasons, both business and pleasure. These days I even take the videos people want me to review on my iPod to watch on the plane. There is a lot of video material at BT; people will video a process, or the way a system works, and ask me to comment on it. Or I will look at a communication video that has been shot and I will check it to see whether I like what's been said. But generally the iPod is a relaxation tool.

So those three are there all the time. They are all very active. Now in a big customer service organization operating across the world like mine, where somebody is working 24 hours a day, the technology is good for increasing responsiveness at a time when our customers need us to be very responsive. That is excellent. But it is pretty bad for giving me thinking time. If I let it, it will stop me taking blocks of time to talk to people or think through things with people, or just think through things on my own. And I think the danger that I would recommend everybody watches out for, is that it could prevent you from having thinking time. You can't be a good leader unless you allow yourself to have enough thinking and planning time. I think it's crucial.

And how do you do that?

You just refuse to take the technology with you into meetings or similar types of situation. You have to cut yourself off, and make sure that you have people around you who can deal with urgent issues when you're not doing it.

Because you've got the technology, and because they know what sort of a man you are, do people expect instant responses to emails and texts?

Yes, often those who work closely with me in particular get very used to instant responses. That is good at one level. I operate on a global basis so I do a lot of travelling and there is a lot of time going into and out of airports when you can keep the business running with very low overhead costs to yourself. Filling dead time up is one of the things I like to do and technology really helps with that.

But time management is much more important in other ways. In a very senior role, there is a lot of management to do. You use a big chunk of your time taking part in the management team of your boss (in my case in the board of BT), another in your own management team, and making sure that your people know what they are doing and that their performance is reviewed, and so on. And that's a lot of time. Then you will almost certainly spend a sizeable chunk of time on external things: It could relate to customer activity (in my case, it is heavily customer-oriented) but might also relate to shareholders or people – the set pieces or the communication activities that you do. I then leave a lot of time for what I call 'issues' …

And is that what you referred to earlier as 'thinking time'?

No, thinking time would be a combination of issue time and the time I spend with my management team or with the board of BT, because some of that is done collectively, and some of it is done on your own.

'Issue time' is, for example, when we are in the middle of considering an acquisition, and I would want to go and meet the management team; or we have a particular customer problem. I sometimes go right down into the detail if I think I can get my organization to learn something by me doing it. I often encourage people to escalate what seems like a very small problem, if it's an illustration of a class of problem, because by giving a demonstration of how an issue can be resolved you can make a significant difference.

In your personal development, thinking about how you spend your time is a very important thing to do. How much is work? How much is home, or whatever else you do? How much is development and networking time? How much time are you going to choose to spend on each? How much time do you spend on management tasks such as customer and people issues? Do you leave yourself some time for what is urgent? Do you accept that some of your time has to be spent on tasks that vary from time to time? I find people get trapped into the way they run their time. I do too. I have to have people close to me who will force me to change the way I operate my time, otherwise I like to be available to everyone and talk to all sorts of people about many things. You have to force yourself to decide quite carefully how you use your time.

I am sure that no two days are the same, but do you devote time at the beginning of the day to plan how much time you are going to spend on each element during it?

No. I think most senior people live their lives in 15-minute blocks, with very, very little ability to exercise much change during the day without letting people down. One of the things I've discovered is that as you become more senior, at least 80 per cent of your meetings are more important for the person who is meeting you, than for you. But for you to help them and get full value you have to be respectful and give them equal importance. So we have to plan further in advance than each day. Normally I would plan two or three weeks in advance in detail. Some things are planned months and months in advance, like board meetings and things like that. Two or three weeks in advance in detail, and then as you get closer at the beginning of the week, or more likely the end of the previous week, you can assess the urgent issues that have arisen, and that's when you get disruption and you have to knock out meetings. But if you are knocking out things in the middle of the day, that's very disruptive on other people. I would always try to avoid that.

I think very senior people don't get a lot of blank spaces in their diaries. But maybe it's a personal choice because some people do it very well! I don't work alone particularly well. I tend to work better in groups.

Finding time for 'management by walking about' is also very important. I think if you have got a factory then that is pretty obvious. But walking about offices is kind of a weird thing to do! But getting clear input from people at all levels in your organization, in an environment where they feel they can communicate with trust, is very important. And that's what I mean by 'walking about'.

There are lots of structured ways you can achieve this. I do things called '12 at 12s' where we just get 12 people around the table and we use what is called the 'Chatham House Rules': we can talk outside the meeting about what was said, but we can't say who said what. We just have 12 people around the table at 12 o'clock. Well actually it's often ten people at one o'clock, but the principle is the same! Whenever I am visiting a city, anywhere in the world, I try to do a small meeting with a group of our people of all levels.

Will there be any agenda?

No agenda. I just say, 'What do you want to talk about?' The point about that is that that gives me a set of inputs. I tell them that there will be no action points for me out of this. It just gives me information. Similarly, I make time to go on visits where we talk in detail about what work people are doing. But I think in most very big organizations you have to plan these things carefully. I also do open forums. They give you a different perspective than small groups because people mainly want to hear and understand and often people, depending on their culture, will not raise the more difficult issues. You are much more likely to hear difficult issues in the smaller groups.

While we use electronic communications when we can, a part of my time is spent getting input that wouldn't come about unless I was there in person. For example, there is virtually nothing so valuable to a business as spending time with customers. One of the reasons I travel so much is that, in the end, it is almost impossible to be aware of what a Chinese customer really wants without going to see a Chinese customer in China. In any case, I think that there is a leadership responsibility around presence. We use electronic communication for calls and video conferencing, but there is something enormously motivating for a team, and interesting to the press, amongst other things, about you being present in a particular location. So there is a need to balance all of that.

But I can't over-emphasize the importance of thinking about what you are doing with your time. When we talk about personal growth, I think that one of the most important things to do whenever you get a new job is to really *think* about time. In my case, I am not disciplined enough to make changes without support. So I need to have a colleague who will work with me to make sure that I don't say yes when I should have said no.

Managing yourself mentally

Andy Green had been talking about managing time, and had stressed the importance of building thinking time into one's routine, particularly when one takes on a new position or role in an organization. Yet his last comment had surprised me. He had said: 'In my case, I am not disciplined enough to make changes without support. So I need to have a colleague who will work with me to make sure that I don't say yes when I should have said no.' Andy has been with BT for almost 21 years, and had been Chief Executive of BT Global since 2001. What makes someone with that experience want or need a support network around him? It surely can't be a lack of confidence? What would it be? I had to ask him.

I would say, when we talk about managing yourself mentally, that I don't think there are any perfect leaders. Everybody has very significant weaknesses. Good leaders build teams around them who deal with their weaknesses. So they are prepared to say, 'Look, I am not very good at that', and then make sure that they have somebody on the team who can deal with those issues for them. I have to manage myself to change. There are people who say I am relaxed – one or two people might even say I'm lazy! – that is a misunderstanding I think, but it is very, very important for me to recognize that I need more organizational support around me than other people do.

That is what makes a difference to you?

If I am going to be effective I have to use my time correctly, so I need that support. I also need people around me who are strong deliverers of concepts. I am strategy-led in the way I operate. I think about the future and try to work out an intercept path which gives us an advantage, and then I can drive the organization in that direction. So I work best with individuals who will take an idea from me, work it out and come back to me and say, 'This is what we are trying to do'. Then we might have another good debate, and finally they will go off and do it. Those sorts of people are people who work better with me than the more wavy-handed strategists; although I need a few of them to tell me I'm stupid when I'm going off in the wrong direction! With them, I can have a good row working out what the issues are.

It is crucial that you think about what you're strong at, and how you build a team of people who are capable of delivering, because if you believe you are going to do it yourself, you are nuts. I run a 30,000-strong organization and if all the decisions come to me then we are going to move at a snail's pace. So in my world, I am trying to get hundreds of people scattered across the globe who, given a situation, will think as close to the way I would think about it as possible. They will take responsibility, they will take a decision, they will move on. And I am trying to get enough communication amongst us all so that they don't go off and do exactly the opposite of what I would want to do in that situation. It is about having a shared mental model.

So there has got to be empathy?

Absolutely – 'What are we all trying to do?' I think what gives you power in an organization is the ability to build a culture that creates shared understanding and purpose. And that's another reason for being out and about, for spending time with people. It is a crucial issue I think.

Crises

When I met Andy Green for the first time, he had mentioned to me that he regarded managing oneself mentally as a vital skill for any aspiring manager or leader. I had already learned that part of that involved being mature enough to recognize your own shortfalls, and accept that you are not going to be able to do everything yourself. But what other skills make you mentally fitter to manage?

I have learned myself, and I would advise anyone keen to develop their career, to 'run towards the fire'. There's nothing like dealing with the biggest crisis you can find to learn about pace, organizational change and ambition. And let's face it, you are hardly likely to make a bad situation worse! It's a great learning experience. A crisis will demonstrate to you the people who you can rely on in the world and will also teach you the most valuable management skills. A lot of people walk away from crises. If you are ambitious, my advice is to get in there and help out. In tense situations, you develop true networks, people who you know you can work with over long distances and over a long period of time.

Is there a particular crisis that moulded your career?

My career was built on something called payphones. I was on the point of leaving BT because I had had enough after about 18 months. My boss then, Duncan Lewis, asked me if I would like to fix the payphones. I was supposed to be doing IT marketing, so I thought that was an interesting concept, and I was given about six weeks to fix a payphone system which had been broken for about 20 years!

It seemed like an impossible task. The payphones had been out of action for so long, mainly because customers didn't bother to report them. So even if we fixed them on the day they were reported, we would still miss the target that we had given the government. For years, we had been shouting at the engineers to move faster, but it didn't matter how fast they moved! So the first thing we did was to stop shouting at them, and they loved that.

We still needed a solution to the problem. We realized that we needed to check all the payphones, but how do you go about checking 100,000 public payphones? Eventually, the brainwave came and we found a merchandising company who stocked supermarket shelves. We gave each of their merchandisers a rota of payphones to check, and the problem was solved. Funnily enough, payphones went from losing £60 million to making a £90 million profit, simply because customers could put their money in!

I specialize in the idea of quick response. I honestly believe that a lot of people sit around and wait for long-term solutions to the problems. What do I mean by that? Well, take the issue of the payphones. It was quite clear that the root cause was that the payphones were supposed to self-report, and they didn't. So we could all have sat around and said, 'Well the problem is that the payphones don't self-report'. And we would have worked on that and done nothing else. And in three years' time we would have installed some new payphones, by which time our brand would have been in tatters.

Stress and the work/life balance
Stress is a part of our working lives in the twenty-first century. Few would argue that successful leaders seem either not to

suffer from stress, or they have learned to manage it. Although many who fail to manage their stress effectively endure physical symptoms, the reality is that dealing with stress is largely a mental battle.

I was acutely aware that I was sitting on a sofa alongside one of the calmest people I have ever met. So does Andy Green understand what stress is all about? Does he suffer from it and, if so, how does he manage it?

One of the most important things about stress management is to accept the world as it is. I think most people's stress comes from wishing the world was something else. One of the things I think I am very good at is if, for example, I've got a great player who is on my side and they quit, or I have invested a long time in a contract or a piece of M&A (mergers & acquisitions) and it goes away, then I get over it. I might be grumpy for 30 minutes or need a glass of wine in the evening, but I am over it. The next day I am thinking about what's next, and I am not looking back. I think that you reduce your stress level enormously by living in the real world as it is today and by keeping up with it.

The other thing that reduces stress is believing you are in control. Now you may say this is delusion, but I always say to my children, 'Try to do unto the world, not to be done unto'. This is not meant in an aggressive way at all, rather it is about a mental attitude. If you say, 'This is my problem, I have chosen to do this work, it is my job to employ everybody around me to get the right result', then you feel as though you are in control of the situation and you plan and think your way through it. The times I have seen people get most stressed (and I try to get my managers to understand this) is when you put people in a situation where they have no choice. For example, saying to someone, 'You have got to come in and work on Saturday come what may', and they think 'and next Saturday, and one after that' without giving them a sense of the future and giving them no choice in the matter you create stress.

One of the things about my story about payphones is that in situations like that I am painting a picture for everybody that says, 'However hard it may seem now, trust me, this is what is going to happen in the future', and then making that happen. Creating a culture with a sense of, 'You follow me, we will all do this together and however difficult it may feel right now, there is an answer at the end' – I think that reduces everybody's stress.

But it is also about how you can give people some control, and this is true about work/life balance as well. Work/life balance is not, in my mind, about the number of hours you spend in one place or in another place. What matters to people is, if you really need to be at the school gate at 4.30 p.m. on a given day, or every day then you can do that even if you work loads of hours in the evening. What stresses you is the inability to be able to be at the school gate on time – it is not about how many hours you are being asked to do, rather it's the inflexibility of those hours. So for different people at different times, what actually constitutes the stress point between the home and their work is very different. And you know, we don't talk about it. How many times does a manager sit down with the people they are responsible for and ask, 'What really matters to you at home? When I am arranging meetings and things like that, what should I watch out for you? How can I help you feel better?' It is often the smallest things. I personally don't think this is about work/life balance, it is about how we all understand each other's stress points and how we can avoid them.

And, from what I understand, about what matters to people?

What matters to *individuals*. Somehow that needs to be assessed in individual conversations and we need to be more respectful. For example, when you are sitting in a project team meeting and Fred has disappeared, we need to be respectful that that's Fred's point of pain. However, if he's always away then that's another issue altogether. But we do need to be respectful.

The other thing I believe about work/life balance is *being there*, mentally. I think the worst thing I can do is to turn up at home with my mind still full of work and not listen to a word of what's being said around me. I went through a period of quite significant rows at home with the family because I would walk in, not very early anyway, and I would not be completely with them.

So what changes have you made that have enabled you to arrive home and accept that you can switch off now?

Deliberately thinking it through and deciding that was what I was going to do. On occasions now, I will stay away when I don't actually need to be away from home, just because I am so hyped up with a load of stuff that I know if I go home it is just going to cause chaos. But when I am at home, I am actually doing the things that I am supposed to be doing at home and not doing things that I am supposed to be doing at work.

So let's just pursue that for a minute. You get home, you have opened a bottle of wine, you have switched off, and then your pocket vibrates because your Blackberry has received an email. What do you do?

My Blackberry doesn't vibrate ... although my phone does! If my phone vibrates then I will probably answer it because it could well be a personal call. So I will check who it is, and depending on what the situation is at home I might or might not take the call, but I would think about it very carefully. In terms of my Blackberry, I find it a good thing, especially when I am on holiday. Being able to receive emails stops me having lots and lots of phone calls because 20 minutes of emailing on the Blackberry at the end of an evening, or the end of a day when you are on holiday, can clear 90 per cent of things. You can decide for yourself whether there is anything that really needs to be done, because you are not having to keep phoning people back. If my daughter hadn't grassed me up, I think nobody would ever have known that I had a Blackberry, but she is too observant of these things!

But regarding work/life balance ... to be honest with you, the technology does matter and people talk about it a lot. One of the techniques I espoused at this year's World Economic Forum, when I presented to a workaholics seminar, was not to take your Blackberry battery charger on holiday. It is quite feasible to go two weeks on one battery on a Blackberry as long as you only turn it on for 20 minutes a day. I said that if you really, really can't do it, then I don't advise just cutting yourself off completely, because you then just end up making phone calls which are much more disruptive in my view. So these are just some little techniques you can try.

But that is just technology. The other aspect is the human aspect. The worst conversation I have probably ever had was with my now 13-year-old, who was six at the time. He said, 'Dad, your boss is so horrible, he makes you work so hard …' and I sat down with the whole family and said, 'Look guys, we have all got to understand that dad works hard because he loves work. I go to work because it is great for us all, for our standard of living and all those things, but I am basically there, because I am happy when I'm at work, and when I come home I want to spend time being with you. But if I mix the two things up it doesn't work very well. I've got a big job which I love but you really can't blame my boss, because my boss never tells me what to do'. Nobody tells you what to do at senior levels, you are deciding these things for yourself. So my advice is, if you have got to work at the weekend, decide what time you are going to work, tell everybody that's the time you are working, and then don't work after it. Don't let it drift on throughout the weekend.

And have you stuck to that?

I stick to it mainly. You know, I had a very busy week last week, and I sat down in the garden working on paperwork for a lot of Sunday. It was all right because everybody was busy, and when they came up to me, I stopped. But it is not ideal. I would personally prefer to do less and less of that sort of thing. I try to avoid long periods of weekend working if I possibly can, because it is pretty busy the rest of the time.

I think one of the challenges of people discussing the work/life balance is that they see a balance as the same amount of each. They assume that if you

have got too much of one then you haven't got enough of the other ...

I think it is about managing yourself mentally. I think you have to decide for yourself – it is quite selfish – what is right for you. I really think it is important that we respect each other on this sort of thing. What worries me mainly is setting an example. I think some senior people often set the worst example because they set up a pattern in people which says that the only way you can succeed is by working lots and lots of hours.

So what do you think about organizations that instil a long hours culture?

They worry me. On the other hand, it would be impossible for me personally to say that I am going to work nine-to-five because that's a better example for everybody. I would I hate it, it would drive me absolutely nuts. Somehow, we have to find a way to communicate about these things amongst ourselves.

Just to recap on the stress side, what I have heard is that you must take responsibility, live with the present, forget the past. If something has happened, accept it and move on.

The final thing I would say about it, is that it is much easier to be less stressed if you have a relationship with your boss that has a good degree of trust in it. I argue creating that trust is my problem – I don't argue it is my boss's problem.

If you want a trusting relationship with your boss, then sitting there and waiting for your boss to create a trusting relationship with you is not what I would recommend. Personally, as part of wanting to be in control to reduce my stress levels, I have always taken it as my responsibility to manage my boss – to understand what is important to them, to work on that, to make their life as easy as possible, and to create a relationship where, if I am in a point of great uncertainty or things are very tough they will support me. I will stand in for any of my people at the drop of a hat and hope my boss will do the same for me. If it gets to the point where, for one reason or another, something can't be done – whether it is a personal thing or a work thing – they would turn up for a meeting for me. I will turn up at a meeting for my people, and I think that this helps with making people feel in control. I think this is a very big issue. It is a bit like the Hawthorne experiment that I always remember from my A levels, when you install something which allows people to stop the conveyor belt when they are working on a production line and they all produce much better work, feel much better, even though they don't ever pull the thing. I think there are deep psychological lessons in that for us all about being in control.

The other thing I would say about stress and senior management is that while some people would call me relaxed, I would say I am calm. The worse a situation gets, the more in crisis it becomes, the more I try to be a centre of purposeful calm. I do not want to be screaming and shouting and sending out random instructions. I don't want to be putting too much pressure on places where you can tell the pressure is already hot enough – there is no more they can reasonably do. So I am consistently trying, as things get tougher and tougher, to be more and more thoughtful, rational, calm and reassuring to people about what has to be done – often quite forceful and directive in moments of crisis, but not spreading pandemonium and stress, because I don't think that helps get you out of crisis

.

What I am hearing is that one of the key ways to do that is to accept the crisis.

Absolutely.

And would you say that in some crises the people who are stressed are people who are effectively trying to fight the crisis?

I think that as a manager you have to accept that what you do makes a big difference, so you can easily stress your teams out. And you have a bit of a problem if you are in a very large organization. I know that we are very results-driven, that I am a very results-driven person, and that creates enormous pressure down through the organization – not because of screaming and shouting, but just because everybody knows that that is what the place is all about. If you get to a weak manager then that can very quickly create stress for those underneath that manager, because a weak manager at a time of crisis or poor results will very often create confusion. Bad things get done in your name every day when you run a very big group. There is no doubt about that. But I think we can all work at this to help each other on this strategy.

I also ask my people to look out for each other. One of the things I continually do is say, you don't have to be in a boss relationship to look out for people, you can look out for each other.

And you would endorse that both professionally and personally?

Yes, absolutely. I think it is often quite difficult to spot stress in personal situations, but my guess is that well over 50 per cent of situations where people are seriously stressed at work are not actually primarily related to the work. They may be related to some part of work, but they are almost certainly primarily to do with their personal life. So people get stressed, I think, rather than work makes them stressed. And they get stressed for lots of reasons. Life is tough for lots of people in lots of ways.

Perhaps that is really where the attention for dealing with work/life balance tension should be focused?

I think many people can help each other. One of the things about a good organization is when peers look out for each other and help each other, particularly in an organization like mine where lots of people work in very diverse ways in different places around the world. So people you work with directly may not even be in the same town or even in the same country, but you will always be in some sort of work group, and so that type of thinking is quite important.

Managing yourself physically

When Andy Green told me that he thought he managed stress quite well, he is obviously right. He then added, 'I also often have a lot of adrenaline', as if this was a very good thing. I was a little surprised. My memory from Biology class at school was that adrenaline was essential for our 'fight or flight' response – the example given always seemed to involve our ancestors running away from some large carnivorous animal. In a modern business context, I can appreciate that adrenaline is great for getting something done. However, my understanding is that having lots of adrenaline in our bodies, which we don't do something with, is not good for us at all. So I asked Andy how he deals with it, and how he gets rid of it at the end of the working day?

I don't. I like to have a lot of adrenaline.

But clearly by the time you get off a train or get out of the car at the end of the day you have got rid of it, haven't you?

There is that I suppose. I think I am able to move things from the front to the back of my mind quite well. You can work off adrenaline on the trampoline if you want as well, or whatever you do with the family. But I would say the point about adrenaline is that I like to be under pressure. So I like it when we have got difficult things to do and we have got a lot of people to convince, I love that sort of stuff. I thoroughly enjoy getting involved with anything which is enabling the team really to drive forward, or where I can make a very significant personal contribution. It is great. Going out on a pitch with a sales team is a great thing to do.

But is the opposite true of you? What are you like if you've got too much time before an event?

Yes, I am a good 'first take' person – on a video, a second take is not likely to be as good as the first. But I think people are very different in those sorts of ways.

So would you consciously put off doing something because the adrenaline, the pressure, isn't yet there?

No, I like to be organized. You need to be confident that all the information you need is going to be there. I couldn't present my way out of a paper bag at 25, I was basically shy. And of course when you go into a very senior job you are not just presenting, you are on show all the time. That was quite tricky. It took me quite a long time to get used to it.

I think everybody should try to understand what they are good at. For example, I have a very slow patch in the afternoon. I am capable of sleeping on planes, getting off planes, going straight to work, working flat out, getting on another plane, and I haven't a problem with that sort of stuff. I can manage my jet lag. But if I am in the UK under normal situations, around two o'clock is not a good time to have a one-to-one with me. I am likely to nod off in front of you. I just have a very low physical battery. Some people are great in the morning, some people are great in the evening. People have different physical cycles, and you need to know them. The biggest problem I find is when you have got a poor relationship with someone and you need to make it better, and you've got different cycles is finding the right time to try to rebuild the relationship.

One other reason why people don't get on well in relationships is because some people think very fast and some people think much slower, not because they are less good thinkers, they just like to think things through and mull them over. If people have different cycle speeds, they find it very difficult to create a partnership that really works.

Returning to the question of how you manage yourself physically: I like to keep fit, not very fit, but fit enough. I have back problems and other things which I need to manage.

So is there a gym here?

There is a gym here, but I don't use it. I did yoga and now Pilates, and I think it is important to understand your diet and what you drink or don't drink. Some people drink alcohol and feel fine, but you need to know when and how you can do various things, when should you eat, when should you not eat. Particularly if you are running an international business environment, if you don't know how to manage yourself into sleeping when you have to be asleep and not sleeping when you don't, it makes the whole job much more difficult. Now you don't have to do it like I do, by filling the whole day. There are people I know who get off a plane and they need two hours either to rest or exercise, depending on who they are, but if they set their agenda up properly they are fantastically effective. Other people you find are almost crumbling around you because they are trying to keep up and just can't. If you are going to be in a senior position, particularly a global one, managing yourself physically is something everybody needs to think about. If you need down-time – take it. You just have to find ways around it. Now you can't always, but if it's a real adrenaline situation, mostly you'll get through it anyway, most people do. But I think that you do need to understand physically what you need to do.

I used to work in north-west London, and if my MD was in trouble we always knew because he would go for a walk in the Chiltern Hills. He'd be back in two hours, but he would drive off to High Wycombe and go for a climb in the hills.

Absolutely. Personally I think that is underrated. What do I think are the things that most correlate with people getting to the top? A will and a desire to get there. There is a correlation in intelligence. We have talked about dynamism, this sort of questing sense – and the physical ability to do it.

And from what you're saying, the 'physical' isn't just exercise, it's diet, it's sleep ...

Yes, it is all the things that work for you.

Managing your growth

Andy Green had mentioned to me before the interview just how important he thought the issue was of managing one's personal growth inside an organization, and throughout one's career. As you take on more responsibility in an organization, what should you do differently? From a personal perspective, I have witnessed a number of very good workers who are promoted to management positions, and who then fail. Why is this? Andy takes the issue very seriously.

The biggest mistake I see people make is that they go up a level in an organization, or they get a more senior position, and they don't change what they do.

So what changes are necessary? What advice would you offer someone whose role and level of responsibility was growing inside an organization?

If you consider the issue of managing growth, it brings a number of threads together. I think this is probably one of the most important things for individuals to think about.

One of the pieces of advice I always give to people is that if you are a manager who wishes to grow, or take on more responsibility, then you need to look at what your role comprises. It's very rare in today's information world for someone only to be doing management. You will also have your own set of tasks to perform. And I would say that whatever tasks you are responsible for, make sure you do them very well. That is priority number one.

Secondly, you need to develop yourself as a manager. Learn the skills of a manager. Learn how to make the people who are working for you effective.

Thirdly, try to help your boss do a great job. Help your boss, and they, in turn, will be thinking about the role you are performing in a much wider context.

And the final thing is this idea of what at Shell we used to call 'helicopter'. Are you somebody who is able to rise above what you are doing? Can you see the environment, the customers, the technology changes, the company, and say, 'Well, actually, we should be doing something different here'. What's significant is that you are not focusing solely or narrowly on your own personal objectives, you are thinking about how dynamically you can change what is going on around you and how you and your role fits in with everyone else's.

Shell called it 'helicopter'. It sounds similar to the NLP (Neuro-Linguistic Programming) technique of looking at a situation from a number of different positions or perspectives?

Absolutely. And I think it is really important, this ability to place what you are doing in context. It's one of those things that sets people apart. Some try to do it while forgetting the first three points. You tend only to get away with that when you're young, because business people are inclined to forgive a bit at the start of your career, and so they should.

But that leads to the next important point: Mistakes are excellent for learning. You can learn so much when you make a mistake. I have personally found that that is particularly true of mergers and acquisitions. Every time you go into a merger and acquisition transaction and decide not to do it, you still need to treat it as a success and a learning opportunity. It can be very hard for a team because they have usually spent a lot of time on it, and then you decide that you are not going to do it. There are lots of situations like this, and they create fantastic learning opportunities.

And how about recruitment? Does the sort of people you should recruit change as you grow in an organization?

When people move into a new role, generally they continue to recruit the same sort of people they had in their last role. They don't say, 'I need somebody who is like I was two years ago, a different level of person'. Very often they find it quite difficult to recruit people at the right seniority because they have been promoted up through an organization. Particularly somebody like me who has stayed with one organization a long time – people remember you and they may say, 'What's he doing up there?' And therefore you have to put particular energy and effort into doing the right things. And that includes, as you get older, asking yourself what are the right external things for you to be doing – which conferences should you speak at, which dinners you should go to, all those types of things – as well as how you spend your time internally on what you do, how you project the position you are in.

It is really surprising how often that is at the heart of people who are doing really, really well, and then they suddenly stop. They have taken on a new set of responsibilities, they are still great people, they are doing their task very well, but underneath them they don't have the structure and they are not positioning themselves externally and inside the organization in a manner which enables them genuinely to take on that role. Sometimes it is about doing it but not feeling quite comfortable with the people they are now peers with, and so mentally re-adjusting yourself to your position all the time as you go through your career is an extremely important part of what you need to do.

So you are newly promoted, and you have got new responsibilities, new levels of management. Two or three tips – where would you start?

I would start with my time. I would start with saying, 'Who are the most important people whom I have to work with to get done what I have got to do?' I would make a conscious effort to make sure that I was operating at the right level. Not because I am status-conscious – but because I am in a position to influence people at a certain level. That is part of what happens in life. Personally, I never lose my network of people at all levels in the organization because they are tremendously useful. I always say to people when they stop working for me, you haven't really stopped working for me, I am just lending you away for a while. Now if you are supposed to be running a sales team of 200 and you are still going and seeing the same customers, and the same people are still coming to the rugby with you or whatever else, you are doing the wrong thing. You are representing your company, you should have a new group of contacts and you should be entertaining different people. That is an obvious example, but it actually occurs very often. So I would emphasize that very strongly.

The second thing I would say is that the first time you come to change your team, watch yourself like a hawk. The crucial thing is to try to recruit somebody better than yourself. Now nobody likes this. I have done it always. I have always tried to recruit people who are better than me, if not in everything, then at least in some things. A good plan, if you want to be really successful, is to have great people wanting to work for you and doing fantastic work. I personally would like to be sitting at home as much as possible doing nothing, so I think if I can find great people to do the work then I don't have to worry about it, because I know the results are going to come through and they are going to do it with good values, and do it well. Hey, that's fantastic! But the number of people who think, 'Oh I'd better not, they might show me up' – people working for you don't show you up, not if you are a good manager.

How far into your career did it take you to learn that?

I was in my mid to late thirties before I became aware that this is a big issue. I think that is partly because I was doing lots of fixing things. I didn't tend to have very big teams, I was leading across the organization rather than dealing with teams. I think it was just one of those growing-up things.

We talked earlier about the importance of networking and building your own network. Have you always been a good networker?

No, in fact I'm a bit of a loner. I'm still not a great networker. However, one of my great strengths is reading a room. So from a very early age I used to have to go and present to the board on all sorts of things, and I would work out what I thought the positions of the various directors were going to be.

What form would that take?

I would research the individuals. I am the same when I work with the sales force today. I would research them and understand what they are like, understand what sort of angle they might come from, and then after the third or fourth time presenting to them you would know them a bit.

I start with going in with as much information as possible, but then the crucial thing is to *listen*. It still stuns me how often I will come out of a meeting with one of my sales people and their reading of the meeting will be very different to mine. Even now. And I look at them and I think, how could you possibly have thought that? Listening to what is not said in a meeting is very important, and it is something that some people don't seem to be able to do. The thing that I feel sets aside really top-level negotiators and some top-level leaders from other people is that they can understand what is going on in the other person's head. We have all been to those meetings where somebody has turned up with you and they have gone off in the wrong direction and done completely the opposite of what you would have chosen to do. And it is remarkable how many meetings go like that. You can be quite well prepared, and still find that one side or the other has gone off on a tangent and you have to find a way to pull things back on track.

Specifically it is about understanding the context of everybody in the room, and about increasing the precision of your listening skills. Very thoughtful listening: what are they saying, why are they saying that and not something else, and what are they not saying? It is hugely important, particularly in an international environment because you have then got an awful lot of cultural aspects to consider.

I was going to ask you that because presumably, in an international meeting, is must be tempting to attribute periods of silence to just a difference in culture?

There are all sorts of issues around that. If you go to a translated Chinese or Japanese meeting you are in a completely different world, and there are all sorts of different things to worry about when you are in a global environment.

But the same rules apply?

The same rules apply, I think, in the sense that you should try to practice really listening to people. As somebody once said to me, listening without preparing to reply. I don't know about you, but because I am quite an active person, if somebody starts saying something to me, they will be half-way through the sentence and I'll be thinking of what am I going to say next. But if you can actually spend some time listening to people and try to understand what they are saying properly, and then think about your reply, it may be a bit slower than you might normally be, you might even put in a couple of fluffy phrases to get your act together, but it is worth practising.

My own experience is that there are an awful lot of business situations where people seem unable to bear silence.

It really is worth practising – 'Am I really hearing what these people are saying, do I really understand where they are coming from?' Because I think it is still an underrated skill, and I think too few people are very good at it. If you have got a personal situation which is not going well, then you absolutely have got to try to shake yourself out of thinking of the person when they walk into the room, and instead really listen to what they are saying. If you're thinking, 'Well Joe didn't deliver for me last week, and I heard he said something nasty about me in the corridor the week before ...', when Joe opens his mouth, whatever he says, you have got that big tail of baggage, and the result is that you get these very locked relationships which you can't unlock.

I talk to people a lot about the 'prisoner's dilemma'. Sometimes I have to instruct my team, when they are in some confrontational position with another company or another department that we are going to assume a good response when we hold out an olive branch. We are going to assume a good response and we are going to drop our guard, and even if they come back and we get a slap around the face, we are going to do it again. I might change my mind after a few slaps around the face! But I think an enormous problem in both business situations between organizations, and particularly between individuals, is to break out of deadlocked positions, the need to break negative relationship cycles. Trying to unlock situations which are not going well by deliberately saying, 'I will accept that part of what is happening here is that I am seeing Joe through these glasses which are just filled up with all this negative stuff and therefore we are never going to break out of this' is an important technique. So take that on board, go into a meeting, one-on-one, and just turn it around to be a positive by saying, 'I am going to keep an open mind, I am going to think positively about this person and situation'.

Very easy to say, and you have clearly managed to master it, but for someone who finds it difficult to disregard the baggage and forget it, what would you suggest?

I have not found it easy to do that. Although I do find it easy to leave the past behind in terms of what has happened in the world, actually leaving the past behind around people is much harder for me. So I carry the baggage around of what people have done to me or I have done to people. One of the things that this is about is guilt, because very often these blockages come most because you have been unfair to someone and you feel guilty about it. So sometimes it is not something the other person has done, it is something you've done, but nevertheless it sets up these blockages between people. So I find it quite easy to end up in locked positions – unlocking them has very high value.

But it doesn't necessarily come naturally?

It doesn't come naturally, so you have to sit down and decide that you are going to do it. Now I use coaches, not in the same way as most people talk about coaches, but if I feel that I need to spend some time developing my relationship with some peers or with some colleagues or customers, I will pick someone to sit down and talk through the problem with. So if it is a team issue, I will pick somebody from the HR department who is in that area and we will have a really clear conversation about what I am feeling.

I am a great believer that you are more likely to change and be thoughtful about what you are doing if you share it with someone. I am going to go away on a team-building thing in a couple of weeks time with my team, and one of the things I will do at the end of it is say, 'OK, this is the contract I've got with you guys is a result of today. I am going to try to make these changes. I am asking, you to pick me up when I don't do it.'

Now some people find that very threatening in a way, but why if you have got enough confidence in yourself and you really want to improve? I find that you need a friendly colleague who will say, 'Didn't you say you were not going to do that to people, didn't you say you were going to make that clearer?' One of the things people say about me, because I think a lot and talk very fast, is that I am not always very clear. So a very simple technique is to have somebody who can say to you, 'I really didn't understand that Andy', and for it not to be an issue, or for either of us to feel threatened by it. But rather where people are able to say, 'Yes, that's in the contract, we all agreed. We all know Andy's a bit fuzzy around the edges because he thinks in different circles, so let's batter this until we all really understand it because we'll be better as a team once we have.'

So the tip here is, if you are trying to develop yourself, share it with someone who you are prepared to discuss it with.

And be brutally honest about it?

Yes, be really honest. I am a strategically led person, but we have a house rule among the strategy team in BT Global services: they are absolutely allowed to tell me that they think I am talking rubbish, because it's that challenge that creates a lot of value.

So when someone picks you up on something, does it annoy you, or do you welcome someone challenging you?

I am like any other person. Depending on the basis of the challenge, usually it is fine. However, there are some people I wouldn't dream of authorizing to do it. You need to think about who is going to be saying it to you!

Managing your image

Earlier in our discussion, Andy Green had recounted a piece of advice he had been given about why he wasn't always treated by his colleagues with the seniority that his position merited. I asked Andy to tell me more.

One of the best pieces of advice I ever got was when I walked into my then boss's office and asked him why people didn't treat me as the Strategy Director of a FTSE 30 company? And he said that if I want to be treated like one, then I should act like one. And it was very straightforward. I think it was one of the four pieces of advice that have stuck in my mind over the years, because often we don't take on the necessary attributes of our new roles very quickly.

This piece of advice prompted a wider discussion about the importance of 'image' – though Andy was quick to point out that he was referring to the word in the context of the way that managers or leaders present themselves.

I think that one of the things we really need to be careful about, and which we haven't talked about yet, is that I think you have to be true to yourself to be a good leader. I think people know when you are not genuine very quickly.

Are we talking about you personally here, or just anyone?

Anyone. When I was trying to learn how to do presentations, it was terrible. I was reading the books and I was going on the courses and trying to do it that way, and eventually I had someone from the theatre, a dramatist, who came and worked with me on it – and she said, this is never going to work. You have got to tell a story, and you have got to tell it from your own personal point of view. And as soon as I absorbed the idea that I displayed my own personality when on the stage or anywhere else, then it started to come together. I tell it as a story. I will often stop in the middle of something and say, 'When I was thinking about this, the key issue here was with this', and then suddenly you have got a completely different Andy standing on the stage than somebody who is just reading a slide. So we each have to be true to ourselves.

I also believe that it is very hard to be a really good leader if people don't believe you are committed to the enterprise, to the journey, to the company, whatever it is. In fact, I think it is difficult to get good followership if people think you are in it only for the money.

I see that. But Andy, there must have been times when there was a change or a process where you thought, I just don't believe in this – what do you do then?

That's very interesting. This is the question about whether you want to be a shop steward or a leader? There is an aspect to this question relating to values. If something happened in the company that really compromised my values, I would leave. I have no hesitation about that and I would think most people you talk to would agree with that. But I frequently find myself at the wrong end of a decision, something I think is wrong.

And you then have to carry that decision forward?

The question is, 'What do I then do about it?' When I was younger I used to go in and say 'Stupid bastards, blah blah blah'. And that's what I mean by shop stewards. The shop steward manager listens to all the things people are saying, and then when they are delivering the message further down the chain, they discuss whether it is a good thing or a bad thing within the little group for which they are responsible. And what happens there is that you end up with people being more stressed because, if you think about it, they are not doing what I said earlier: they are not living in today's world. A decision has been made, but they are saying, 'Now wouldn't it be better if that decision hadn't been made'. And the leaders are not helping their people change their world in line with that decision.

So what I say to leaders, and what I try to do myself, is to accept a decision, communicate it, work out what it means for us, and get on with our lives. That's it. We don't then think about whether it was the right or wrong decision. The world is always interesting and things unravel sometimes, but that is what you have committed to do. So one of the things I say to lots of people is, 'That's the policy'. And they might say, 'Well it's the wrong policy'. My reply is, 'OK, let's go and work out if it's the wrong policy, and if it's the wrong policy, we'll change it. And then we will tell everybody about the new policy. But until we have changed it, that's the policy'.

Another important question is how to help people who have an issue. Do you give them an answer or help them find an answer? I mentioned earlier the '12 at 12s'. I don't take any action points myself, but I will say to people, if I was faced with that problem I'd do these sorts of things, go talk to that person, do this, that and the other. The alternative approach is to say, 'Well look, we have given so-and-so the task of leading this, I think your job is to get alongside them and make your concerns known to them, but you know, if that is the direction we are going in, make sure it works for us as an organization'.

I think good leaders are continually trying to give their team a sense that they are in control, that they are living in the now, and therefore they are taking in decisions coming from the organization from all directions.

Not all of which they will agree with.

Not all of which they'll agree with, but I think there is a huge difference between living with things you don't agree with and not living to your values. For example, there are some things that worry me a lot, such as the security of our people in different parts of the world. I really don't think anybody can instruct me to do anything I don't want to do in that area and expect to keep me in the company.

For example, I operate in 170 countries. I am sure some of my agents somewhere are doing some things which I personally would not approve of – it would be very difficult to believe that that wasn't happening. So where's the edge? The edge for me is commitment to making sure that everybody understands what is expected. If you see anything, deal with it. It's about trying to make sure that your audits and other checks capture the things that they should, trying to live your values in the real world. You can't, as I said, in a 30,000-strong organization assume that everything will be done by the book every day, but you can send a clear signal that you expect things to be done by the book.

So my view is that you have to ask yourself, 'Are you living in the real world? Are you a force for what you consider the good?' And as long as you are confident that your presence in the organization has a positive effect, then you should stand by. But there are times when your value set prompts you to say, 'I'm off, because I am not going to be associated with a company that does that'.

Are those times pretty clear-cut?

I think they are clear-cut in today's high disclosure environments. Particularly as a board director I think you know when your values are seriously compromised, and you absolutely need to deal with it. But that's different from expecting that every part of your organization should reflect your value set. You know, I like working in telecommunications environments, I think it is generally a good thing in the world. I think IT and communications are a positive thing, so that sits quite well with me. But if you get to be in a very senior position, you can't guarantee that every part of your organization is running according your value set, all the time. You can try to make that happen, but you won't always succeed. So I think that all you can do is decide for yourself whether you are prepared to be a leader, but if you do, then you do take responsibility if something goes wrong, and you will have to make decisions that aren't always comfortable.

I sense that the biggest tip you would give to someone who is growing in an organization and progressing through an organization is to be true to yourself in terms of recognizing your values, is that right?

Not just recognizing your values – I think you need to develop a style which is true to yourself. I think good leaders, great leaders, show their personality. They don't try to make themselves into a mannequin – there are lots of those around, but they are not the great leaders in my view. The great leaders are the ones who people feel they know. People have heard them speak, and they feel they know a bit about them.

Conclusions and recommendations

Andy Green is a straightforward, unshowy man. His biography doesn't run into several pages of public awards, memberships or committees. Instead, his achievements speak for themselves. He has earned his position by delivering remarkable bottom-line success for one of the world's best known companies over a 21-year period.

Part of his achievement can be attributed to his remarkable people skills, which I had witnessed first hand. Here was a man who had told me that he didn't like the questions I had prepared, and had provided me with an alternative question structure in their place. From anyone else, that might well have irritated and unnerved me. Not so with Andy Green. In fact, using Andy's structure provided a logical and sensible progression for our discussion, and I was grateful to him.

Andy's approach to managing yourself considers five key topics: managing your time; managing yourself mentally; managing yourself physically; managing your image; and managing your growth. He has plenty to say on each, although he was quick to point out that everyone is different. Managing your time, for example, is about taking stock of where you are at, and building in opportunities for thought, for planning and for issues. Managing yourself mentally is about accepting the world as it is. Do that, he says, and you instantly have the tool you need to manage stress effectively. It's also about accepting your limitations and being mature enough to build an effective support network around you. Managing yourself physically is not necessarily about pumping iron every morning, it's about knowing what your body needs to perform, and then providing plenty of it. Managing your image has nothing whatever to do with playing a role. It's about being yourself, about taking responsibility and about making sure that your people know you, your strengths and your limitations. Finally, managing your growth is about all of these things, and especially about recognizing that you have to change the way you work, the way you recruit and the way that you manage as you progress through your organization.

Managing yourself checklist

If you are assessing how best to manage yourself as a leader, here are some issues to think about. You might want to find a few, valuable minutes to take a clean sheet of paper and jot down any ideas that the following list generates.

Dynamist
Do you question everything? Are you always looking for a better way of doing things? Do you accept that you have to change?

Managing time
How well do you think you manage time? What role, if any, does technology play in the way that you manage time? Do you allow yourself enough thinking time? Planning time? Issue time? Do you ever stop and think about how you spend your time? Would you say that your work life and home life are well balanced? Are you 'trapped' in the way that you manage your time? Do you manage by 'walking about'? Would introducing '12 at 12s' work for you?

Managing your mental state
What are your strengths and weaknesses? Who around you can support you in the areas of weakness you have identified? Could you reduce the stress in your role by 'accepting the world as it is'? Andy Green stays fresh by constantly changing his working environment – what could you do to 'keep the world looking different'? Would you say

that you are in control? What really matters to you at work? What really matters to you at home? If you suffer from stress, how much of it do you bring into the office from home, and how much is work-related? Do you understand what causes your people's stress? When your working day is done, and you are at home, can you switch off? Are you 'being there'? Are you a workaholic? Could you leave your Blackberry charger at home for a fortnight?

Managing your physical side

Are you someone who is always pumped up with adrenaline? How do you use it effectively? Are you a 'first take' person? What is your best time of day, when you are most effective? What do you do to keep fit? Do you understand physically what you need to do? How is your diet? How well do you sleep?

Managing your growth

How have you changed as you have grown through your organization or career? Are you still recruiting the same sort of people? What effect would recruiting someone better than you have? Have you stopped to consider what your role actually comprises? How does your role fit in with that of your colleagues? Have you paused to think about how you could help your boss do a good job? Are you good at 'moving on'? In a disagreement, are you good at leaving the 'baggage' behind? Do you use coaches, either formally or informally? Do you share issues with other people, or are you determined to work them through yourself? How do you feel if someone challenges you?

Conclusion by
Ed Peppitt

Leading people

So what have we learned about how best to lead people from Sir Michael Bichard? Sir Michael outlined how the first step involves creating a sense of purpose, a vision if you prefer, of what you and your organization intend to achieve. It was interesting to hear how challenging it is to criticize a team member for failure to deliver, if you have not played your part in creating the team's direction or purpose in the first place.

Next, you have to give people ownership of the vision. Sir Michael described as 'exciting' the moment when people get to the point where they are using their own initiative to deliver.

Third, you need to lay out a very clear set of values. Values are as important as the vision, because through values you influence behaviour. When you have a sense of purpose or a vision, and you combine it with a set of values, then you know not only where the business is going, but also how your people will work together to get there. Sir Michael's own values all relate to the way that you treat and respect the people that you work with.

To lead people well, you need to communicate effectively. Sir Michael's approach to effective communication centred on making himself available to as wide an audience as he could. In larger organizations, this involved publicising when he was available and where, so that people could take time to come and discuss issues with him. In smaller organizations, he would arrange coffee mornings, tea breaks and other opportunities to meet his team and talk with them. He talked about the importance of really *listening* to what people had to say, and also about putting yourself into someone else's shoes to get a feel for what their experience was like.

He talked about how he has always tried to 'remove obstacles' to win people over, and to demonstrate that he has understood their problems. Removing obstacles is a good way, he said, to 'create energy' amongst your people, a term he prefers to the more generic 'motivation'. All this has been central to Sir Michael's approach to leading people because it has proven to be the most effective way to create and grow a strong team around you. His approach has always been to lead teams of people with a very flat hierarchy, with their informality enhanced by a healthy injection of humour.

So much for the principles of leading people. If we are responsible for a team of people, we should give thought to our own vision and values, and how we might give our people ownership of them. We need to consider how effectively we communicate with our people, and where we could improve. However, Sir Michael's overriding principle is that a good leader must demonstrate absolute integrity. *You have to be yourself.* For that reason, it is vital that you take the Sir Michael's principles of leading people, but then apply them in your own way. If it isn't natural for you to communicate with your people through a series of coffee mornings, then for goodness sake don't do it. You will be found out before the Digestives have been passed around. The important thing to note is the need to communicate. How you do it must come from you.

The same applies for all the principles Sir Michael discussed. He has established a set of values at the University of the Arts, based around quality and customer service. There's no point whatever in simply applying those same values to your organization. You need to think about what values best represent you. Flatter hierarchies, injected with a little informality and humour, have served Sir Michael well. They may well be the ideal way to create motivated and energetic teams in your organization. But not necessarily. Give some thought to how to create a strong team around you, but be flexible enough to appreciate that copying Sir Michael's tactics won't necessarily deliver the same results.

As I mentioned in the introduction, this book is not a blueprint for how to manage and lead. It's more of a signpost. Adopt the principles that our leaders suggest, by all means, but remember, above all else, to be yourself.

Managing change

I thought that one of the most interesting insights that Sir John Tusa offered was that he hadn't appreciated the extent of the problems at the Barbican before he took up the post. In fact, he said that he didn't believe that 'anybody who goes into an institution ever has any real idea of what the nature of the problems are'.

Managing change effectively involves many of the skills endorsed by Sir Michael Bichard's approach to leading people. After all, having identified the extent of the problems, the challenge rests with leading your people through the change programme that you will inevitably implement. You need good people around you, who will support and lend weight to your proposals for change. But others will find the programme stressful, and Sir John's advice is to be bold and stand firm throughout the difficult period that you implement change.

Change isn't something you implement without very good reason. You need to develop a strategic plan for change. Sir John's position was unusual in that he knew that his plan would never be accepted, so he broke it down into a series of smaller, more tactical proposals. Nevertheless, the bigger picture was there from the start.

Given that stress and distrust breed when changes occur, communication is an essential skill. For Sir John at the Barbican, this meant introducing general and team meetings periodically throughout the year. They were sufficiently successful for many new suggestions for improvement and change to come from the very people who would otherwise fear change the most. Effective communication within the Barbican was also achieved through recruiting a new group of team leaders with a broad remit of skills and responsibilities. The result has been a flatter hierarchy, with much more responsibility being pushed downwards to more junior staff.

Finally, managing change effectively concerns recognising

the need for change in the first place. In Sir John's case, the fact that he needed a lot of persuading that a change was necessary meant that sometimes the change was implemented a little later than his colleagues would have preferred.

From listening to Sir John, it would be easy to conclude that the principles of managing change are straightforward, even if they are tough to implement. However, that conclusion would be simplistic because, like Sir Michael Bichard before him, much of his approach is invested in his personal values. The best example is that, by his own admission, Sir John thrives on the stress and pressure of his work. It's well documented that many people find any organizational change stressful, but he is not amongst them. If you don't thrive on the stress and pressure of your role, it's highly unlikely that you will be able to implement change by modelling the same tactics as Sir John. Instead you need to look at the principles that he discussed, and consider how you could best adopt them yourself.

Looking at your own people, how could you encourage them to create and drive the momentum for change? How effectively have you communicated with your people during periods of change in the past? What could you do better next time? From the way Sir John talked about his team leaders, it sounds as if he is prepared to delegate a lot of responsibility downwards. Would you be happy to do that? If you did, what sort of reporting would you need? A monthly written report, or a daily phone call? As I have said before, this book is a guide to good practice, rather than a blueprint. The principles that our leaders suggest are thoroughly sound. How you implement them, however, must come from you.

Meeting customer needs

Meeting the needs of your customers is vital to an organization's survival, particularly if the organization in question is attempting to bring a brand new product to a market with which they have no experience or knowledge. That's precisely what Karan Bilimoria did when he established Cobra beer just over a decade ago.

The principles of meeting your customers' needs can be summarized succinctly. Good business ideas are almost always customer-driven, and often come from being dissatisfied with an existing product or service. You need to understand as fully as possible what your customers need or want, so extensive research is essential. In Karan Bilimoria's case, this comprised research into the market, the brewing process, the sales and marketing channels, as well as the product itself. In marketing terms, he says, you are looking for a niche in the market, and a market in the niche, and that's what he saw with the opportunity for a premium, less gassy lager.

There are several other elements that mark his approach to meeting customer needs. However good your product, effective sales skills are vital, and will set you up throughout your career in business. I was interested to hear Karan talk about the need for constant innovation. Cobra is established and has been phenomenally successful, but the company still takes every opportunity to innovate. Etching a pictorial history of the company onto the beer bottles is hardly necessary, but it's a good example of how Cobra has remained fresh, interesting and innovative. Karan refers to it as the need to 'zig' when those around you 'zag'.

As with most areas of management or leadership, effective communication skills are a must. For Karan, this includes internal as well as external communication. Cobra communicates with its customers through its advertising, and through the surveys and feedback that the company encourages. However, it's internally where Karan has clearly made an equally sizeable impact. Every one of the people at Cobra are ambassadors for the company and the brand, and it seems like a great place to work. It was interesting to hear that Karan will meet up with his staff, sometimes from all over the country, to catch up and to share a drink after work on a Friday evening. There can't be many organizations whose people are prepared to drive into West London on a Friday evening for a catch up with the boss, but Cobra is one.

One of the most significant requirements that Karan discussed seemed almost a paradox. It's the need to identify what customers need or want, even if they are not aware of the need themselves. Perhaps the best illustration of this was when Karan introduced beer in bottles that all his customers told him were too large, and would not suit the British market. Karan persevered anyway, and Cobra's customers soon adapted with willingness and enthusiasm.

At one level it is easy to put together a shortlist of the key principles that Karan Bilimoria endorses to meet customer needs effectively. Research your market, communicate well, be prepared to polish up your sales skills and be innovative. It sounds straightforward on paper, but talking to Karan quickly makes you realize that there is a whole lot more. One could be forgiven for thinking that on the basis of Cobra's beginnings, the most important requirement is just to back yourself and follow your gut instinct. But that would be far too simplistic. Remember that Karan Bilimoria was a qualified accountant and lawyer at the time Cobra started. Much of the preparation and planning would have come very naturally to him.

Just as with Sir Michael Bichard and Sir John Tusa, I realized during the course of the interview that Cobra's success can be largely attributed to the integrity of its founder. Karan is driven and quite charming. And he is his own man. His excitement and motivation are infectious. If he had chosen to, I am sure he could have persuaded me to go out and sell a crate or two of Cobra there and then. I can see why his staff and his customers are such strong supporters. What this means, however, is that Karan has found ways to meet customer needs that work for *him*. He has applied the principles in his own way, and that is what we must all do.

Effective communication is essential, but calling in your staff for a catch up on a Friday evening will almost certainly not work for you. What could you do to improve communication in your organization? Being able to predict what your customers want, when they don't know it themselves, can give you a substantial competitive advantage. But you will need every ounce of Karan's charisma and determination to force a size, colour or type of product onto your customers, when they have expressly stated that they don't want it! So just as with leading people, and managing change, the important lesson to take away from Karan Bilimoria is to take on board the principles that he identifies, and then consider *how* you might best implement them yourself.

Managing information and knowledge

Sir Digby Jones outlined how the development of the British economy over the last ten years has resulted in the need to handle, process and manage ever increasing amounts of information. From a personal perspective, Sir Digby has addressed this through ruthless management of himself: He reads prodigiously, he delegates effectively and he prioritizes well.

In fact, the most effective ways to manage information and knowledge are largely personal ones, according to Sir Digby. You need to be able to deal with stress. I was interested and encouraged by his distinction between stress and pressure. One must learn to accept and deal with pressure, but stress is pressure over which you have no control, and you must do whatever it takes to overcome it.

It was also interesting to note how much focus Sir Digby was prepared to give to the issue of relaxation, and learning to balance the competing pressures of work and home. Getting the work/life balance in perspective is vital if you are going to keep on top of information and knowledge. Sir Digby works hard, but he will make time for himself, even if it means catching up with four episodes of Spooks back to back. With a national culture of working long hours, it was refreshing to hear him state categorically that he always takes his full holiday entitlement, no matter what. There's a lesson for us all there. If you work long hours, or decline to take holidays, you should ask yourself why? Is it out of necessity, or because you feel under pressure to do so? The vital principle is to get the balance between work and home working effectively for *you*.

We have learned how important it is to delegate effectively. For Sir Digby, that means having a strong team around him, who are aware of his strengths and limitations. He has chosen to delegate responsibility for his diary and his email, which works well for him, particularly as it means that he no longer feels tied to a laptop that accompanies his business travels. The principle of delegation for effective management is a sound one, but not everyone would benefit from delegating responsibility for email. The important questions are, how good are you at delegating, what could you delegate and to whom?

You can't delegate effectively without a strong team around you, and Sir Digby had plenty to say about the importance of people. Communication is key, but so is creating a working environment where people are encouraged to work together. One tactic that works for Sir Digby is to keep his office door open at all times, and to acknowledge, loudly, when he has made a mistake! By doing that, he says, it encourages others to be open about their shortcomings, and to work hard to do something about them. Would bellowing out apologies for your mistakes work for you? What else could you do to create a culture of teamwork and responsibility?

Managing activities and resources

It was interesting to note that Dianne Thompson regarded her people as her most valuable resource and that she, like Sir Digby at the CBI, has worked hard to create a positive, energetic culture at Camelot. The energy and motivation come very easily to Dianne, mainly because she has clearly found her ideal role. She is absolutely serious when she says that she gets up each morning to go to work to make Britain a better place. It may have taken almost six years to achieve, but she is justly proud that the culture at Camelot can be likened to a stick of rock. Slice any Camelot employee inside and they are like a stick of rock that says 'Camelot' or 'National Lottery' all the way through. There is a family culture at Camelot, which is clearly Dianne's own. How would your organization fare if you tried to instil a culture of one big, happy family? What cultural values might suit your own organization better?

Creating an effective culture is just one of Dianne Thompson's guiding principles for managing your people, your most valuable resource. You must be open, transparent and you must communicate well. For Camelot that has meant introducing specific measures for cascading information up and down through the organization in a hurry. Dianne never wants to face a situation again where staff find out what is going on, not from Dianne herself, but from watching the news on television.

Dianne Thompson's measures for efficiency have come about from necessity. Camelot only see half a pence profit from every pound spent on the lottery, so it's vital that every efficiency measure is in place. She has introduced systems to Camelot that measure the effectiveness of every marketing pound spent, and calculate and report on their return. Are you as disciplined in your organization? What measures of efficiency could you introduce?

Managing yourself

It was a measure of how well Andy Green manages himself that he had identified so clearly what he wanted to discuss. Managing yourself comprises five distinct elements: managing your time, managing yourself mentally, managing yourself physically, managing your growth and managing your image.

Managing time encompasses many of the conventional methods recommended in books and on courses, but also some exceptional ones. Building in thinking and issue time is essential, for example. Most interesting of all is Andy's method for getting clear input from people at all levels of BT. His '12 at 12s' get a dozen people around a table to discuss the issues of current concern. We all know about the need to manage time effectively, but what would work best for you? Do you give yourself thinking time and, if not, how could you start to do so?

Andy regards running headlong into a crisis situation, and dealing with it, as absolutely ideal training for managing yourself mentally. Certainly being charged with the mission to repair the defunct payphone network in six weeks was a challenge that set Andy up for the rest of his career. Recognizing the need for mental fitness is an important principle, though how you achieve can only come from you. For Andy, dealing with a crisis is effective. What about you? Managing yourself physically is a similar principle. For some of us, it means daily workouts in the gym. For others, a walk in the woods a couple of times a week. For Andy, it's yoga. What about you?

Managing your growth throughout your organization and career is an absolutely vital principle, and one which Andy believes many people fail to appreciate. When people take on new responsibilities, or go up a level, they don't change their approach or behaviour. You need to learn not to simply recruit the same or similar people to work for you. Instead you must recognize your changing needs and requirements, and recruit the very best people for the job. Managing yourself mentally is important as you grow. Andy's example was a great one: If you want to be treated like the strategy director of a FTSE 30 company, then you need to act like one. What changes do you need to make yourself?

Integrity

Having interviewed the six leaders, it was inevitable that I would start to look for methods or attitudes that all six adopted, whether spoken or unspoken. It was clear that there are no shortcuts: not one of the leaders could have sustained their position of leadership successfully if they had not acquired and then followed sound management principles. However, what struck me is that all six discussed their belief in the importance of openness, integrity or of 'being yourself'.

There are a few noteworthy examples. Sir Michael Bichard voiced that integrity is essential if you expect to lead a team of people effectively. People need to know where you stand. They may not always agree with you, but if you are open and straight with people, they will tend to support and respect your decisions regardless. Dianne Thompson was even more emphatic on the subject. The lottery has to be open, honest, fair and beyond question. The day there is doubt about the integrity of Camelot, then the decline of the lottery will begin. And Sir John Tusa also endorses the need for openness and integrity when introducing and managing strategic change. If people trust and respect you, then the impetus for change will come straight from the people who are affected most by it.

I don't know why I am surprised that all six leaders regard the issue of openness and integrity as so important. In many ways, I am hugely heartened. I suppose it is partly due to the rather formulaic approach that so many management books and courses take. They don't always factor in the need to 'be yourself'. It's also partly due to the portrayal of managers and leaders on television. 'The Apprentice' is a case in point, but there are other examples. There was a series recently where three employees had to spend a week sucking up to their boss, and feeding his ego. One of them won a promotion at the end of the week. Television like this seems to fly in the face of the principles that my six interviewees outlined.

Being yourself, however, also means that many of the specific tactics that the six leaders recommended might not actually work for you. I hope it is clear that the principles of management and leadership outlined are what we should be following. How we deliver them is up to us.

Six passionate people

There is one other characteristic that all six leaders displayed. Some even talked about it. They are all absolutely passionate about what they do. Three leaders argued that if you aren't passionate for what you do, then you must leave your organization and find out what you are passionate about.

Karan Bilimoria has many skills and qualifications, but Cobra would not have got off the ground without his passion for his product and his passion to make it succeed. It is so deep-rooted that he was even prepared to try out various other businesses whilst specifically waiting for the right opportunity to set up Cobra. It was his passion that saw Cobra through difficult times, and it was the same passion that came across, and continues to come across, to his customers.

Dianne Thompson's passion for leading Camelot is so strong that I honestly can't imagine what she might otherwise do. She fears that it sounds naff, but she really means it when she describes her role as helping to make Britain a better place. Sir Michael Bichard voiced his support for passion quite clearly:

'I think one of the other things that all of the leaders I respect have had have is a passion and a belief in what they are doing in the organization, in the product, in the service.'

No one is suggesting that if you have passion on its own, you will automatically be a successful leader. You will still need the knowledge, skills and experience that underpin good management and leadership principles. However, passion is what sets people apart, and there is a strong case for searching for a career or vocation that you are passionate about. I have a friend who buys run-down properties at auction, renovates them and then sells them as a decent property on the open market. Almost everyone who meets her for the first time comes away thinking that they want to be a property developer. In fact, they don't. They just want to feel as passionate about something as my friend is about developing properties. So what might that be?

I really hope that this book has given you a number of ideas to think about in your management career. Having been given the wonderful opportunity to meet and interview six such extraordinary people, I hope that I have captured some of their wisdom on the printed page. The principles of management are there for you to follow, but I hope that you will add to them the integrity, passion and determination to make your success absolutely guaranteed.

Index